RAGGED LADY

Part 1

William Dean Howells

Ragged Lady, Part 1

William Dean Howells

© 1st World Library, 2006
PO Box 2211
Fairfield, IA 52556
www.1stworldlibrary.com
First Edition

LCCN: 2006935364

Softcover ISBN: 1-4218-2509-0
Hardcover ISBN: 1-4218-2409-4
eBook ISBN: 1-4218-2609-7

Purchase *"Ragged Lady, Part 1"*
as a traditional bound book at:
www.1stWorldLibrary.com/purchase.asp?ISBN=1-4218-2509-0

1st World Library is a literary, educational organization dedicated to:

- Creating a free internet library of downloadable ebooks

- Hosting writing competitions and offering book publishing scholarships.

Interested in more 1st World Library books?
contact: literacy@1stworldlibrary.com

Check us out at: www.1stworldlibrary.com

1ˢᵗ World Library Literary Society

Giving Back to the World

"If you want to work on the core problem, it's early school literacy."

— **James Barksdale, former CEO of Netscape**

"No skill is more crucial to the future of a child, or to a democratic and prosperous society, than literacy."

— **Los Angeles Times**

Literacy... means far more than learning how to read and write... The aim is to transmit... knowledge and promote social participation."

— **UNESCO**

"Literacy is not a luxury, it is a right and a responsibility. If our world is to meet the challenges of the twenty-first century we must harness the energy and creativity of all our citizens."

— **President Bill Clinton**

"Parents should be encouraged to read to their children, and teachers should be equipped with all available techniques for teaching literacy, so the varying needs and capacities of individual kids can be taken into account."
- Hugh Mackay

I

It was their first summer at Middlemount and the Landers did not know the roads. When they came to a place where they had a choice of two, she said that now he must get out of the carry-all and ask at the house standing a little back in the edge of the pine woods, which road they ought to take for South Middlemount. She alleged many cases in which they had met trouble through his perverse reluctance to find out where they were before he pushed rashly forward in their drives. Whilst she urged the facts she reached forward from the back seat where she sat, and held her hand upon the reins to prevent his starting the horse, which was impartially cropping first the sweet fern on one side and then the blueberry bushes on the other side of the narrow wheel-track. She declared at last that if he would not get out and ask she would do it herself, and at this the dry little man jerked the reins in spite of her, and the horse suddenly pulled the carry-all to the right, and seemed about to overset it.

"Oh, what are you doing, Albe't?" Mrs. Lander lamented, falling helpless against the back of her seat. "Haven't I always told you to speak to the hoss fust?"

"He wouldn't have minded my speakin'," said her husband. "I'm goin' to take you up to the dooa so that you can ask for youaself without gettin' out."

This was so well, in view of Mrs. Lander's age and bulk, and the hardship she must have undergone, if she had tried to carry out her threat, that she was obliged to take it in some sort as a favor; and while the vehicle rose and sank over the surface left rough, after building, in front of the house, like a vessel on a chopping sea, she was silent for several seconds.

The house was still in a raw state of unfinish, though it seemed to have been lived in for a year at least. The earth had been banked up at the foundations for warmth in winter, and the sheathing of the walls had been splotched with irregular spaces of weather boarding; there was a good roof over all, but the window-casings had been merely set in their places and the trim left for a future impulse of the builder. A block of wood suggested the intention of steps at the front door, which stood hospitably open, but remained unresponsive for some time after the Landers made their appeal to the house at large by anxious noises in their throats, and by talking loud with each other, and then talking low. They wondered whether there were anybody in the house; and decided that there must be, for there was smoke coming out of the stove pipe piercing the roof of the wing at the rear.

Mr. Lander brought himself under censure by venturing, without his wife's authority, to lean forward and tap on the door-frame with the butt of his whip. At the sound, a shrill voice called instantly from the region of the stove pipe, "Clem! Clementina? Go to the front dooa! The'e's somebody knockin'." The sound of feet, soft and quick, made itself heard within, and in a few moments a slim maid, too large for a little girl, too childlike for a young girl, stood in the open doorway, looking down on the elderly people in the buggy, with a face as glad as a flower's. She had blue eyes, and a smiling mouth, a straight nose, and a pretty chin whose firm jut accented a certain wistfulness of her lips. She had hair of a dull, dark yellow, which sent out from its thick mass light prongs, or tendrils, curving inward again till they delicately touched it. Her tanned face was not very different in color from her hair, and neither were her bare feet, which showed well above her ankles in the calico skirt she wore. At sight of the elders in the buggy she involuntarily stooped a little to lengthen her skirt in effect, and at the same time she pulled it together sidewise, to close a tear in it, but she lost in her anxiety no ray of the joy which the mere presence of the strangers seemed to give her, and she kept smiling sunnily upon them while she waited for them to speak.

"Oh!" Mrs. Lander began with involuntary apology in her tone, "we just wished to know which of these roads went to South Middlemount. We've come from the hotel, and we wa'n't quite ce'tain."

The girl laughed as she said, "Both roads go to South Middlemount'm; they join together again just a little piece farther on."

The girl and the woman in their parlance replaced the letter 'r' by vowel sounds almost too obscure to be represented, except where it came last in a word before a word beginning with a vowel; there it was annexed to the vowel by a strong liaison, according to the custom universal in rural New England.

"Oh, do they?" said Mrs. Lander.

"Yes'm," answered the girl. "It's a kind of tu'nout in the wintatime; or I guess that's what made it in the beginning; sometimes folks take one hand side and sometimes the other, and that keeps them separate; but they're really the same road, 'm."

"Thank you," said Mrs. Lander, and she pushed her husband to make him say something, too, but he remained silently intent upon the child's prettiness, which her blue eyes seemed to illumine with a light of their own. She had got hold of the door, now, and was using it as if it was a piece of drapery, to hide not only the tear in her gown, but somehow both her bare feet. She leaned out beyond the edge of it; and then, at moments she vanished altogether behind it.

Since Mr. Lander would not speak, and made no sign of

starting up his horse, Mrs. Lander added, "I presume you must be used to havin' people ask about the road, if it's so puzzlin'."

"O, yes'm," returned the girl, gladly. "Almost every day, in the summatime."

"You have got a pretty place for a home, he'e," said Mrs. Lander.

"Well, it will be when it's finished up." Without leaning forward inconveniently Mrs. Lander could see that the partitions of the house within were lathed, but not plastered, and the girl looked round as if to realize its condition and added, "It isn't quite finished inside."

"We wouldn't, have troubled you," said Mrs. Lander, "if we had seen anybody to inquire of."

"Yes'm," said the girl. "It a'n't any trouble."

"There are not many otha houses about, very nea', but I don't suppose you get lonesome; young folks are plenty of company for themselves, and if you've got any brothas and sistas -"

"Oh," said the girl, with a tender laugh, "I've got eva so many of them!"

There was a stir in the bushes about the carriage, and Mrs. Lander was aware for an instant of children's faces looking through the leaves at her and then flashing out of sight, with gay cries at being seen. A boy, older than the rest, came round in front of the horse and passed out of sight at the corner of the house.

Lander now leaned back and looked over his shoulder at his wife as if he might hopefully suppose she had come to the end of her questions, but she gave no sign of encouraging him to start on their way again.

"That your brotha, too?" she asked the girl.

"Yes'm. He's the oldest of the boys; he's next to me."

"I don't know," said Mrs. Lander thoughtfully, "as I noticed how many boys there were, or how many girls."

"I've got two sistas, and three brothas, 'm," said the girl, always smiling sweetly. She now emerged from the shelter of the door, and Mrs. Lander perceived that the slight movements of such parts of her person as had been evident beyond its edge were the effects of some endeavor at greater presentableness. She had contrived to get about her an overskirt which covered the rent in her frock, and she had got a pair of shoes on her feet. Stockings were still wanting, but by a mutual concession of her shoe-tops and the border of her skirt, they were almost eliminated from the problem. This happened altogether when the girl sat down on the threshold, and got herself into such foreshortening that the eye of Mrs. Lander in looking down upon her could not detect their absence. Her little head then showed in the dark of the doorway like a painted head against its background.

"You haven't been livin' here a great while, by the looks," said Mrs. Lander. "It don't seem to be clea'ed off very much."

"We've got quite a ga'den-patch back of the house," replied the girl, "and we should have had moa, but fatha wasn't very well, this spring; he's eva so much better than when we fust came he'e."

"It has, the name of being a very healthy locality," said Mrs. Lander, somewhat discontentedly, "though I can't see as it's done me so very much good, yit. Both your payrints livin'?"

"Yes'm. Oh, yes, indeed!"

"And your mother, is she real rugged? She need to be, with such a flock of little ones!"

"Yes, motha's always well. Fatha was just run down, the doctas said, and ought to keep more in the open air. That's what he's done since he came he'e. He helped a great deal on the house and he planned it all out himself."

"Is he a ca'penta?" asked Mrs. Lander.

"No'm; but he's - I don't know how to express it - he likes to do every kind of thing."

"But he's got some business, ha'n't he?" A shadow of severity crept over Mrs. Lander's tone, in provisional reprehension of possible shiftlessness.

"Yes'm. He was a machinist at the Mills; that's what the doctas thought didn't agree with him. He bought a piece of land he'e, so as to be in the pine woods, and then we built this house."

"When did you say you came?"

"Two yea's ago, this summa."

"Well! What did you do befoa you built this house?"

"We camped the first summa."

"You camped? In a tent?"

"Well, it was pahtly a tent, and pahtly bank."

"I should have thought you would have died."

The girl laughed. "Oh, no, we all kept fast-rate. We slept in the tents we had two - and we cooked in the shanty." She smiled at the notion in adding, "At fast the neighbas thought we we'e Gipsies; and the summa folks thought we were Indians, and wanted to get baskets of us."

Mrs. Lander did not know what to think, and she asked, "But

didn't it almost perish you, stayin' through the winter in an unfinished house?"

"Well, it was pretty cold. But it was so dry, the air was, and the woods kept the wind off nicely."

The same shrill voice in the region of the stovepipe which had sent the girl to the Landers now called her from them. "Clem! Come here a minute!"

The girl said to Mrs. Lander, politely, "You'll have to excuse me, now'm. I've got to go to motha."

"So do!" said Mrs. Lander, and she was so taken by the girl's art and grace in getting to her feet and fading into the background of the hallway without visibly casting any detail of her raiment, that she was not aware of her husband's starting up the horse in time to stop him. They were fairly under way again, when she lamented, "What you doin', Albe't? Whe'e you goin'?"

"I'm goin' to South Middlemount. Didn't you want to?"

"Well, of all the men! Drivin' right off without waitin' to say thankye to the child, or take leave, or anything!"

"Seemed to me as if SHE took leave."

"But she was comin' back! And I wanted to ask - "

"I guess you asked enough for one while. Ask the rest tomorra."

Mrs. Lander was a woman who could often be thrown aside from an immediate purpose, by the suggestion of some remoter end, which had already, perhaps, intimated itself to her. She said, "That's true," but by the time her husband had driven down one of the roads beyond the woods into open country, she was a quiver of intolerable curiosity. "Well, all

I've got to say is that I sha'n't rest till I know all about 'em."

"Find out when we get back to the hotel, I guess," said her husband.

"No, I can't wait till I get back to the hotel. I want to know now. I want you should stop at the very fust house we come to. Dea'! The'e don't seem to be any houses, any moa." She peered out around the side of the carry-all and scrutinized the landscape. "Hold on! No, yes it is, too! Whoa! Whoa! The'e's a man in that hay-field, now!"

She laid hold of the reins and pulled the horse to a stand. Mr. Lander looked round over his shoulder at her. "Hadn't you betta wait till you get within half a mile of the man?"

"Well, I want you should stop when you do git to him. Will you? I want to speak to him, and ask him all about those folks."

"I didn't suppose you'd let me have much of a chance," said her husband. When he came within easy hail of the man in the hay-field, he pulled up beside the meadow-wall, where the horse began to nibble the blackberry vines that overran it.

Mrs. Lander beckoned and called to the man, who had stopped pitching hay and now stood leaning on the handle of his fork. At the signs and sounds she made, he came actively forward to the road, bringing his fork with him. When he arrived within easy conversational distance, he planted the tines in the ground and braced himself at an opposite incline from the long smooth handle, and waited for Mrs. Lander to begin.

"Will you please tell us who those folks ah', livin' back there in the edge of the woods, in that new unfinished house?"

The man released his fork with one hand to stoop for a head of timothy that had escaped the scythe, and he put the stem of it between his teeth, where it moved up and down, and whipped fantastically about as he talked, before he answered, "You mean the Claxons?"

"I don't know what thei' name is." Mrs. Lander repeated exactly what she had said.

The farmer said, "Long, red-headed man, kind of sickly-lookin'?"

"We didn't see the man - "

"Little woman, skinny-lookin; pootty tonguey?"

"We didn't see her, eitha; but I guess we hea'd her at the back of the house."

"Lot o' children, about as big as pa'tridges, runnin' round in the bushes?"

"Yes! And a very pretty-appearing girl; about thi'teen or fou'teen, I should think."

The farmer pulled his fork out of the ground, and planted it with his person at new slopes in the figure of a letter A, rather more upright than before. "Yes; it's them," he said. "Ha'n't been in the neighbahood a great while, eitha. Up from down Po'tland way, some'res, I guess. Built that house last summer, as far as it's got, but I don't believe it's goin' to git much fa'tha."

"Why, what's the matta?" demanded Mrs. Lander in an anguish of interest.

The man in the hay-field seemed to think it more dignified to include Lander in this inquiry, and he said with a glimmer of the eye for him, "Hea'd of do-nothin' folks?"

"Seen 'em, too," answered Lander, comprehensively.

"Well, that a'n't Claxon's complaint exactly. He a'n't a do-nothin'; he's a do-everything. I guess it's about as bad." Lander glimmered back at the man, but did not speak.

"Kind of a machinist down at the Mills, where he come from," the farmer began again, and Mrs. Lander, eager not to be left out of the affair for a moment, interrupted:

"Yes, Yes! That's what the gul said."

"But he don't seem to think't the i'on agreed with him, and now he's goin' in for wood. Well, he did have a kind of a foot-powa tu'nin' lathe, and tuned all sots o' things; cups, and bowls, and u'ns for fence-posts, and vases, and sleeve-buttons and little knick-knacks; but the place bunt down, here, a while back, and he's been huntin' round for wood, the whole winta long, to make canes out of for the summa-folks. Seems to think that the smell o' the wood, whether it's green or it's dry, is goin' to cure him, and he can't git too much of it."

"Well, I believe it's so, Albe't!" cried Mrs. Lander, as if her husband had disputed the theory with his taciturn back. He made no other sign of controversy, and the man in the hay-field went on.

"I hea' he's goin' to put up a wind mill, back in an open place he's got, and use the powa for tu'nin', if he eva gits it up. But he don't seem to be in any great of a hurry, and they scrape along somehow. Wife takes in sewin' and the girl wo'ked at the Middlemount House last season. Whole fam'ly's got to tu'n in and help s'po't a man that can do everything."

The farmer appealed with another humorous cast of his eye to Lander; but the old man tacitly refused to take any further part in the talk, which began to flourish apace, in question and answer, between his wife and the man in the hay-field. It seemed that the children had all inherited the father's smartness. The oldest boy could beat the nation at figures, and one of the young ones could draw anything you had a mind to.

They were all clear up in their classes at school, and yet you might say they almost ran wild, between times. The oldest girl was a pretty-behaved little thing, but the man in the hay-field guessed there was not very much to her, compared with some of the boys. Any rate, she had not the name of being so smart at school. Good little thing, too, and kind of mothered the young ones.

Mrs. Lander, when she had wrung the last drop of information out of him, let him crawl back to his work, mentally flaccid, and let her husband drive on, but under a fire of conjecture and asseveration that was scarcely intermitted till they reached their hotel. That night she talked along time about their afternoon's adventure before she allowed him to go to sleep. She said she must certainly see the child again; that they must drive down there in the morning, and ask her all about herself.

"Albe't," she concluded; "I wish we had her to live with us. Yes, I do! I wonder if we could get her to. You know I always did want to adopt a baby."

"You neva said so," Mr. Lander opened his mouth almost for the first time, since the talk began.

"I didn't suppose you'd like it," said his wife.

"Well, she a'n't a baby. I guess you'd find you had your hands full, takon' a half-grown gul like that to bring up."

"I shouldn't be afraid any," the wife declared. "She has just twined herself round my heat. I can't get her pretty looks out of my eyes. I know she's good."

"We'll see how you feel about it in the morning."

The old man began to wind his watch, and his wife seemed to take this for a sign that the incident was closed, for the present at least. He seldom talked, but there came times when he would not even listen. One of these was the time after he had wound his watch. A minute later he had undressed, with an agility incredible of his years, and was in bed, as effectively blind and deaf to his wife's appeals as if he were already asleep.

II

When Albert Gallatin Lander (he was named for an early Secretary of the Treasury as a tribute to the statesman's financial policy) went out of business, his wife began to go out of health; and it became the most serious affair of his declining years to provide for her invalid fancies. He would have liked to buy a place in the Boston suburbs (he preferred one of the Newtons) where they could both have had something to do, she inside of the house, and he outside; but she declared that what they both needed was a good long rest, with freedom from care and trouble of every kind. She broke up their establishment in Boston, and stored their furniture, and she would have made him sell the simple old house in which they had always lived, on an unfashionable up-and-down-hill street of the West End, if he had not taken one of his stubborn stands, and let it for a term of years without consulting her. But she had her way about their own movements, and they began that life of hotels, which they had now lived so long that she believed any other impossible. Its luxury and idleness had told upon each of them with diverse effect.

They had both entered upon it in much the same corporal figure, but she had constantly grown in flesh, while he had dwindled away until he was not much more than half the weight of his prime. Their digestion was alike impaired by their joint life, but as they took the same medicines Mrs. Lander was baffled to account for the varying result. She was sure that all the anxiety came upon her, and that logically she was the one who ought to have wasted away. But she had before her the spectacle of a husband who, while he gave his entire attention to her health, did not audibly or visibly worry about it, and yet had lost weight in such measure that upon trying on a pair of his old trousers taken out of storage with some clothes of her own, he found it impossible to use the side pockets which the change in his figure carried so far to the rear when the garment was reduced at the waist. At the same time her own dresses of ten years earlier would not half meet round her; and one of the most corroding cares of a woman who had done everything a woman could to get rid of care, was what to do with those things which they could neither of them ever wear again. She talked the matter over with herself before her husband, till he took the desperate measure of sending them back to storage; and they had been left there in the spring when the Landers came away for the summer.

They always spent the later spring months at a hotel in the suburbs of Boston, where they arrived in May from a fortnight in a hotel at New York, on their way up from hotels in Washington, Ashville, Aiken and St. Augustine. They passed the summer months in the mountains, and early in the autumn they went back to the hotel in the Boston suburbs, where Mrs. Lander considered it essential to make some sojourn before going to a Boston hotel for November and December, and getting ready to go down to Florida in January. She would not on any account have gone directly to the city from the mountains, for people who did that were sure to lose the good of their summer, and to feel the loss all the winter, if they did not actually come down with a fever.

She was by no means aware that she was a selfish or foolish person. She made Mr. Lander subscribe statedly to worthy objects in Boston, which she still regarded as home, because they had not dwelt any where else since they ceased to live there; and she took lavishly of tickets for all the charitable entertainments in the hotels where they stayed. Few if any guests at hotels enjoyed so much honor from porters, bell-boys, waiters, chambermaids and bootblacks as the Landers, for they gave richly in fees for every conceivable service which could be rendered them; they went out of their way to invent debts of gratitude to menials who had done nothing for them. He would make the boy who sold papers at the dining-room door keep the change, when he had been charged a profit of a hundred per cent. already; and she would let no driver who had plundered them according to the carriage tariff escape without something for himself.

A sense of their munificence penetrated the clerks and proprietors with a just esteem for guests who always wanted the best of everything, and questioned no bill for extras. Mrs. Lander, in fact, who ruled these expenditures, had no knowledge of the value of things, and made her husband pay whatever was asked. Yet when they lived under their own roof they had lived simply, and Lander had got his money in an old-fashioned business way, and not in some delirious speculation such as leaves a man reckless of money afterwards. He had been first of all a tailor, and then he had gone into boys' and youths' clothing in a small way, and finally he had mastered this business and come out at the top, with his hands full. He invested his money so prosperously that the income for two elderly people, who had no children, and only a few outlying relations on his side, was far beyond their wants, or even their whims.

She as a woman, who in spite of her bulk and the jellylike majesty with which she shook in her smoothly casing brown silks, as she entered hotel dining-rooms, and the severity with which she frowned over her fan down the length of the hotel drawing-rooms, betrayed more than her husband the commonness of their origin. She could not help talking, and her accent and her diction gave her away for a middle-class New England person of village birth and unfashionable sojourn in Boston. He, on the contrary, lurked about the hotels where they passed their days in a silence so dignified that when his verbs and nominatives seemed not to agree, you accused your own hearing. He was correctly dressed, as an elderly man should be, in the yesterday of the fashions, and he wore with impressiveness a silk hat whenever such a hat could be worn. A pair of drab cloth gaiters did much to identify him with an old school of gentlemen, not very definite in time or place. He had a full gray beard cut close, and he was in the habit of pursing his mouth a great deal. But he meant nothing by it, and his wife meant nothing by her frowning. They had no wish to subdue or overawe any one, or to pass for persons of social distinction. They really did not know what society was, and they were rather afraid of it than otherwise as they caught sight of it in their journeys and sojourns. They led a life of public seclusion, and dwelling forever amidst crowds, they were all in all to each other, and nothing to the rest of the world, just as they had been when they resided (as they would have said) on Pinckney street. In their own house they had never entertained, though they sometimes had company, in the style of the country town where Mrs. Lander grew up. As soon as she was released to the grandeur of hotel life, she expanded to the full measure of its responsibilities and privileges, but still without seeking to make it the basis of approach to society. Among the people who surrounded her, she had not so much acquaintance as her husband even, who talked so little that he needed none. She sometimes envied his ease in getting on with people when he chose; and his boldness in speaking to fellow guests and fellow travellers, if he really wanted anything. She wanted something of them all the time, she wanted their conversation and their companionship; but in her ignorance of the social arts she was thrown mainly upon the compassion of the chambermaids. She kept these talking as long as she could detain them in her rooms; and often fed them candy (which she ate herself with childish greed) to bribe them to further delays. If she was staying some days in a hotel, she sent for the house-keeper, and made all she could of her as a listener, and as soon as she settled herself for a week, she asked who was the best doctor in the place. With doctors she had no reserves, and she poured out upon them the history of her diseases and symptoms in an inexhaustible flow of statement, conjecture and misgiving, which was by no means affected by her profound and inexpugnable ignorance of the principles of health. From time to time she forgot which side her liver was on, but she had been doctored (as she called it) for all her organs, and she was willing to be doctored for any one of them that happened to be in the place where she fancied a present discomfort. She was not insensible to the claims which her husband's disorders had upon science, and she liked to end the tale of her own sufferings with some such appeal as: "I wish you could do something for Mr. Landa, too, docta." She made him take a little of each medicine that was left for her; but in her presence he always denied that there was anything the matter with him, though he was apt to follow the doctor out of the room, and get a prescription from him for some ailment which he professed not to believe in himself, but wanted to quiet Mrs. Lander's mind about.

He rose early, both from long habit, and from the scant sleep of an elderly man; he could not lie in bed; but his wife always had her breakfast there and remained so long that the chambermaid had done up most of the other rooms and had leisure for talk with her. As soon as he was awake, he stole softly out and was the first in the dining-room for breakfast. He owned to casual acquaintance in moments of expansion that breakfast was his best meal, but he did what he could to make it his worst by beginning with oranges and oatmeal, going forward to beefsteak and fried potatoes, and closing with griddle cakes and syrup, washed down with a cup of cocoa, which his wife decided to be wholesomer than coffee. By the time he had finished such a repast, he crept out of the dining-room in a state of tension little short of anguish, which he confided to the sympathy of the bootblack in the washroom.

He always went from having his shoes polished to get a toothpick at the clerk's desk; and at the Middlemount House, the morning after he had been that drive with Mrs. Lander, he lingered a moment with his elbows beside the register. "How about a buckboa'd?" he asked.

"Something you can drive yourself" - the clerk professionally dropped his eye to the register - "Mr. Lander?"

"Well, no, I guess not, this time," the little man returned, after a moment's reflection. "Know anything of a family named Claxon, down the road, here, a piece?" He twisted his head in the direction he meant.

"This is my first season at Middlemount; but I guess Mr. Atwell will know." The clerk called to the landlord, who was smoking in his private room behind the office, and the landlord came out. The clerk repeated Mr. Lander's questions.

"Pootty good kind of folks, I guess," said the landlord provisionally, through his cigar-smoke. "Man's a kind of univussal genius, but he's got a nice family of children; smaht as traps, all of 'em."

"How about that oldest gul?" asked Mr. Lander.

"Well, the'a," said the landlord, taking the cigar out of his mouth. "I think she's about the nicest little thing goin'. We've had her up he'e, to help out in a busy time, last summer, and she's got moo sense than guls twice as old. Takes hold like - lightnin'."

"About how old did you say she was?"

"Well, you've got me the'a, Mr. Landa; I guess I'll ask Mis' Atwell."

"The'e's no hurry," said Lander. "That buckboa'd be round pretty soon?" he asked of the clerk.

"Be right along now, Mr. Lander," said the clerk, soothingly. He stepped out to the platform that the teams drove up to from the stable, and came back to say that it was coming. "I believe you said you wanted something you could drive yourself?"

"No, I didn't, young man," answered the elder sharply. But the next moment he added, "Come to think of it, I guess it's just as well. You needn't get me no driver. I guess I know the way well enough. You put me in a hitchin' strap."

"All right, Mr. Lander," said the clerk, meekly.

The landlord had caught the peremptory note in Lander's voice, and he came out of his room again to see that there was nothing going wrong.

"It's all right," said Lander, and went out and got into his buckboard.

"Same horse you had yesterday," said the young clerk. "You don't need to spare the whip."

"I guess I can look out for myself," said Lander, and he shook the reins and gave the horse a smart cut, as a hint of what he might expect.

The landlord joined the clerk in looking after the brisk start the horse made. "Not the way he set off with the old lady, yesterday," suggested the clerk.

The landlord rolled his cigar round in his tubed lips. "I guess he's used to ridin' after a good hoss." He added gravely to the clerk, "You don't want to make very free with that man, Mr. Pane. He won't stan' it, and he's a class of custom that you want to cata to when it comes in your way. I suspicioned what he was when they came here and took the highest cost rooms without tu'nin' a haia. They're a class of custom that you won't get outside the big hotels in the big reso'ts. Yes, sir," said the landlord taking a fresh start, "they're them kind of folks that live the whole yea' round in hotels; no'th in summa, south in winta, and city hotels between times. They want the best their money can buy, and they got plenty of it. She" - he meant Mrs. Lander - "has been tellin' my wife how they do; she likes to talk a little betta than he doos; and I guess when it comes to society, they're away up, and they won't stun' any nonsense."

III

Lander came into his wife's room between ten and eleven o'clock, and found her still in bed, but with her half-finished breakfast on a tray before her. As soon as he opened the door she said, "I do wish you would take some of that heat-tonic of mine, Albe't, that the docta left for me in Boston. You'll find it in the upper right bureau box, the'a; and I know it'll be the very thing for you. It'll relieve you of that suffocatin' feeling that I always have, comin' up stars. Dea'! I don't see why they don't have an elevata; they make you pay enough; and I wish you'd get me a little more silva, so's't I can give to the chambamaid and the bell-boy; I do hate to be out of it. I guess you been up and out long ago. They did make that polonaise of mine too tight after all I said, and I've been thinkin' how I could get it alt'ed; but I presume there ain't a seamstress to be had around he'e for love or money. Well, now, that's right, Albe't; I'm glad to see you doin' it."

Lander had opened the lid of the bureau box, and uncorked a bottle from it, and tilted this to his lips.

"Don't take too much," she cautioned him, "or you'll lose the effects. When I take too much of a medicine, it's wo'se than nothing, as fah's I can make out. When I had that spell in Thomasville spring before last, I believe I should have been over it twice as quick if I had taken just half the medicine I did. You don't really feel anyways bad about the heat, do you, Albe't?"

"I'm all right," said Lander. He put back the bottle in its place and sat down.

Mrs. Lander lifted herself on her elbow and looked over at him. "Show me on the bottle how much you took."

He got the bottle out again and showed her with his thumb nail a point which he chose at random.

"Well, that was just about the dose for you," she said; and she sank down in bed again with the air of having used a final precaution. "You don't want to slow your heat up too quick."

Lander did not put the bottle back this time. He kept it in his hand, with his thumb on the cork, and rocked it back and forth on his knees as he spoke. "Why don't you get that woman to alter it for you?"

"What woman alta what?"

"Your polonaise. The one whe'e we stopped yestaday."

"Oh! Well, I've been thinkin' about that child, Albe't; I did before I went to sleep; and I don't believe I want to risk anything with her. It would be a ca'e," said Mrs. Lander with a sigh, "and I guess I don't want to take any moa ca'e than what I've got now. What makes you think she could alta my polonaise?"

"Said she done dress-makin'," said Lander, doggedly.

"You ha'n't been the'a?"

He nodded.

"You didn't say anything to her about her daughta?"

"Yes, I did," said Lander.

"Well, you ce'tainly do equal anything," said his wife. She lay still awhile, and then she roused herself with indignant energy. "Well, then, I can tell you what, Albe't Landa: you can go right straight and take back everything you said. I don't want the child, and I won't have her. I've got care enough to worry me now, I should think; and we should have her whole family on our hands, with that shiftless father of hers, and the whole pack of her brothas and sistas. What made you think I wanted you to do such a thing?"

"You wanted me to do it last night. Wouldn't ha'dly let me go to bed."

"Yes! And how many times have I told you nova to go off and do a thing that I wanted you to, unless you asked me if I did? Must I die befo'e you can find out that there is such a thing as talkin', and such anotha thing as doin'? You wouldn't get yourself into half as many scrapes if you talked more and done less, in this wo'ld." Lander rose.

"Wait! Hold on! What are you going to say to the pooa thing? She'll be so disappointed!"

"I don't know as I shall need to say anything myself," answered the little man, at his dryest. "Leave that to you."

"Well, I can tell you," returned his wife, "I'm not goin' nea' them again; and if you think - What did you ask the woman, anyway?"

"I asked her," he said, "if she wanted to let the gul come and see you about some sewing you had to have done, and she said she did."

"And you didn't speak about havin' her come to live with us?"

"No."

"Well, why in the land didn't you say so before, Albe't?"

"You didn't ask me. What do you want I should say to her now?"

"Say to who?"

"The gul. She's down in the pahlor, waitin'."

"Well, of all the men!" cried Mrs. Lander. But she seemed to find herself, upon reflection, less able to cope with Lander personally than with the situation generally. "Will you send her up, Albe't?" she asked, very patiently, as if he might be driven to further excesses, if not delicately handled. As soon as he had gone out of the room she wished that she had told him to give her time to dress and have her room put in order, before he sent the child up; but she could only make the best of herself in bed with a cap and a breakfast jacket, arranged with the help of a handglass. She had to get out of bed to put her other clothes away in the closet and she seized the chance to push the breakfast tray out of the door, and smooth up the bed, while she composed her features and her ideas to receive her visitor. Both, from long habit rather than from any cause or reason, were of a querulous cast, and her ordinary tone was a snuffle expressive of deep-seated affliction. She was at once plaintive and voluable, and in moments of excitement her need of freeing her mind was so great that she took herself into her own confidence, and found a more sympathetic listener than when she talked to her husband. As she now whisked about her room in her bed-gown with an activity not predicable of her age and shape, and finally plunged under the covering and drew it up to her chin with one hand while she pressed it out decorously over her person with the other, she kept up a rapid flow of lamentation and conjecture. "I do suppose he'll be right back with her before I'm half ready; and what the man was thinkin' of to do such a thing anyway, I don't know. I don't know as she'll notice much, comin' out of such a lookin' place as that, and I don't know as I need to care if she did. But if the'e's care anywhe's around, I presume I'm the one to have it. I presume I did take a fancy to her, and I guess I shall be glad to see how I like her now; and if he's only told her I want some sewin' done, I can scrape up something to let her carry home with her. It's well I keep my things where I can put my hand on 'em at a time like this, and I don't believe I shall sca'e the child, as it is. I do hope Albe't won't hang round half the day before he brings her; I like to have a thing ova."

Lander wandered about looking for the girl through the parlors and the piazzas, and then went to the office to ask what had become of her.

The landlord came out of his room at his question to the clerk. "Oh, I guess she's round in my wife's room, Mr. Landa. She always likes to see Clementina, and I guess they all do. She's a so't o' pet amongst 'em."

"No hurry," said Lander, "I guess my wife ain't quite ready for her yet."

"Well, she'll be right out, in a minute or so," said the landlord.

The old man tilted his hat forward over his eyes, and went to sit on the veranda and look at the landscape while he waited. It was one of the loveliest landscapes in the mountains; the river flowed at the foot of an abrupt slope from the road before the hotel, stealing into and out of the valley, and the mountains, gray in the farther distance, were draped with folds of cloud hanging upon their flanks and tops. But Lander was tired of nearly all kinds of views and prospects, though he put' up with them, in his perpetual movement from place to place, in the same resignation that he suffered the limitations of comfort in parlor cars and sleepers, and the unwholesomeness of hotel tables. He was chained to the restless pursuit of an ideal not his own, but doomed to suffer for its impossibility as if he contrived each of his wife's disappointments from it. He did not philosophize his situation, but accepted it as in an order of Providence which it would be useless for him to oppose; though there were moments when he permitted himself to feel a modest doubt of its justice. He was aware that when he had a house of his own he was master in it, after a fashion, and that as long as he was in business he was in some sort of authority. He perceived that now he was a slave to the wishes of a mistress who did not know what she wanted, and that he was never farther from pleasing her than when he tried to do what she asked. He could not have told how all initiative had been taken from him, and he had fallen into the mere follower of a woman guided only by her whims, who had no object in life except to deprive it of all object. He felt no rancor toward her for this; he knew that she had a tender regard for him, and that she believed she was considering him first in her most selfish arrangements. He always hoped that sometime she would get tired of her restlessness, and be willing to settle down again in some stated place; and wherever it was, he meant to get into some kind of business again. Till this should happen he waited with an apathetic patience of which his present abeyance was a detail. He would hardly have thought it anything unfit, and certainly nothing surprising, that the landlady should have taken the young girl away from where he had left her, and then in the pleasure of talking with her, and finding her a centre of interest for the whole domestic force of the hotel, should have forgotten to bring her back.

The Middlemount House had just been organized on the scale of a first class hotel, with prices that had risen a little in anticipation of the other improvements. The landlord had hitherto united in himself the functions of clerk and head waiter, but he had now got a senior, who was working his way through college, to take charge of the dining-room, and had put in the office a youth of a year's experience as under clerk at a city hotel. But he meant to relinquish no more authority than his wife who frankly kept the name as well as duty of house-keeper. It was in making her morning inspection of the dusting that she found Clementina in the parlor where Lander had told her to sit down till he should come for her.

"Why, Clem!" she said, "I didn't know you! You have grown so! Youa folks all well? I decla'e you ah' quite a woman now," she added, as the girl stood up in her slender, graceful height. "You look as pretty as a pink in that hat. Make that dress youaself? Well, you do beat the witch! I want you should come to my room with me."

Mrs. Atwell showered other questions and exclamations on the girl, who explained how she happened to be there, and said that she supposed she must stay where she was for fear Mr. Lander should come back and find her gone; but Mrs. Atwell overruled her with the fact that Mrs. Lander's breakfast had just gone up to her; and she made her come out and see the new features of the enlarged house-keeping. In the dining-room there were some of the waitresses who had been there the summer before, and recognitions of more or less dignity passed between them and Clementina. The place was now shut against guests, and the head-waiter was having it put in order for the one o'clock dinner. As they came near him, Mrs. Atwell introduced him to Clementina, and he behaved deferentially, as if she were some young lady visitor whom Mrs. Atwell was showing the improvements, but he seemed harassed and impatient, as if he were anxious about his duties, and eager to get at them again. He was a handsome little fellow, with hair lighter than Clementina's and a sanguine complexion, and the color coming and going.

"He's smaht," said Mrs. Atwell, when they had left him - he held the dining-room door open for them, and bowed them out. "I don't know but he worries almost too much. That'll wear off when he gets things runnin' to suit him. He's pretty p'tic'la'. Now I'll show you how they've made the office over, and built in a room for Mr. Atwell behind it."

The landlord welcomed Clementina as if she had been some acceptable class of custom, and when the tall young clerk came in to ask him something, and Mrs. Atwell said, "I want to introduce you to Miss Claxon, Mr. Fane," the clerk smiled down upon her from the height of his smooth, acquiline young face, which he held bent encouragingly upon one side.

"Now, I want you should come in and see where I live, a minute," said Mrs. Atwell. She took the girl from the clerk, and led her to the official housekeeper's room which she said had been prepared for her so that folks need not keep running to her in her private room where she wanted to be alone with her children, when she was there. "Why, you a'n't much moa than a child youaself, Clem, and here I be talkin' to you as if you was a mother in Israel. How old ah' you, this summa? Time does go so!"

"I'm sixteen now," said Clementina, smiling.

"You be? Well, I don't see why I say that, eitha! You're full lahge enough for your age, but not seein' you in long dresses before, I didn't realize your age so much. My, but you do all of you know how to do things!"

"I'm about the only one that don't, Mrs. Atwell," said the girl. "If it hadn't been for mother, I don't believe I could have eva finished this dress." She began to laugh at something passing in her mind, and Mrs. Atwell laughed too, in sympathy, though she did not know what at till Clementina said, "Why, Mrs. Atwell, nea'ly the whole family wo'ked on this dress. Jim drew the patte'n of it from the dress of one of the summa boa'das that he took a fancy to at the Centa, and fatha cut it out, and I helped motha make it. I guess every one of the children helped a little."

"Well, it's just as I said, you can all of you do things," said Mrs. Atwell. "But I guess you ah' the one that keeps 'em straight. What did you say Mr. Landa said his wife wanted of you?"

"He said some kind of sewing that motha could do."

"Well, I'll tell you what! Now, if she ha'n't really got anything that your motha'll want you to help with, I wish you'd come here again and help me. I tuned my foot, here, two-three weeks back, and I feel it, times, and I should like some one to do about half my steppin' for me. I don't want to take you away from her, but IF. You sha'n't go int' the dinin'room, or be under anybody's oddas but mine. Now, will you?"

"I'll see, Mrs. Atwell. I don't like to say anything till I know what Mrs. Landa wants."

"Well, that's right. I decla'e, you've got moa judgment! That's what I used to say about you last summa to my husband: she's got judgment. Well, what's wanted?" Mrs. Atwell spoke to her husband, who had opened her door and looked in, and she stopped rocking, while she waited his answer.

"I guess you don't want to keep Clementina from Mr. Landa much longa. He's settin' out there on the front piazza waitin' for her."

"Well, the'a!" cried Mrs. Atwell. "Ain't that just like me? Why didn't you tell me sooner, Alonzo? Don't you forgit what I said, Clem!"

IV

Mrs. Lander had taken twice of a specific for what she called her nerve-fag before her husband came with Clementina, and had rehearsed aloud many of the things she meant to say to the girl. In spite of her preparation, they were all driven out of her head when Clementina actually appeared, and gave her a bow like a young birch's obeisance in the wind.

"Take a chaia," said Lander, pushing her one, and the girl tilted over toward him, before she sank into it. He went out of the room, and left Mrs. Lander to deal with the problem alone. She apologized for being in bed, but Clementina said so sweetly, "Mr. Landa told me you were not feeling very well, 'm," that she began to be proud of her ailments, and bragged of them at length, and of the different doctors who had treated her for them. While she talked she missed one thing or another, and Clementina seemed to divine what it was she wanted, and got it for her, with a gentle deference which made the elder feel her age cushioned by the girl's youth. When she grew a little heated from the interest she took in her personal annals, and cast off one of the folds of her bed clothing, Clementina got her a fan, and asked her if she should put up one of the windows a little.

"How you do think of things!" said Mrs. Lander. "I guess I will let you. I presume you get used to thinkin' of othas in a lahge family like youas. I don't suppose they could get along without you very well," she suggested.

"I've neva been away except last summa, for a little while."

"And where was you then?"

"I was helping Mrs. Atwell."

"Did you like it?"

"I don't know," said Clementina. "It's pleasant to be whe'e things ah' going on."

"Yes - for young folks," said Mrs. Lander, whom the going on of things had long ceased to bring pleasure.

"It's real nice at home, too," said Clementina. "We have very good times - evenings in the winta; in the summer it's very nice in the woods, around there. It's safe for the children, and they enjoy it, and fatha likes to have them. Motha don't ca'e so much about it. I guess she'd ratha have the house fixed up more, and the place. Fatha's going to do it pretty soon. He thinks the'e's time enough."

"That's the way with men," said Mrs. Lander. "They always think the's time enough; but I like to have things over and done with. What chuhch do you 'tend?"

"Well, there isn't any but the Episcopal," Clementina answered. "I go to that, and some of the children go to the Sunday School. I don't believe fatha ca'es very much for going to chuhch, but he likes Mr. Richling; he's the recta. They take walks in the woods; and they go up the mountains togetha."

"They want," said Mrs. Lander, severely, "to be ca'eful how they drink of them cold brooks when they're heated. Mr. Richling a married man?"

"Oh, yes'm! But they haven't got any family."

"If I could see his wife, I sh'd caution her about lettin' him climb mountains too much. A'n't your father afraid he'll ovado?"

"I don't know. He thinks he can't be too much in the open air on the mountains."

"Well, he may not have the same complaint as Mr. Landa; but I know if I was to climb a mountain,' it would lay me up for a yea'."

The girl did not urge anything against this conviction. She smiled politely and waited patiently for the next turn Mrs. Lander's talk should take, which was oddly enough toward the business Clementina had come upon.

"I declare I most forgot about my polonaise. Mr. Landa said your motha thought she could do something to it for me."

"Yes'm."

"Well, I may as well 'let you see it. If you'll reach into that fuhthest closet, you'll find it on the last uppa hook on the right hand, and if you'll give it to me, I'll show you what I want done. Don't mind the looks of that closet; I've just tossed my things in, till I could get a little time and stren'th to put 'em in odda."

Clementina brought the polonaise to Mrs. Lander, who sat up and spread it before her on the bed, and had a happy half hour in telling the girl where she had bought the material and where she had it made up, and how it came home just as she was going away, and she did not find out that it was all wrong till a week afterwards when she tried it on. By the end of this time the girl had commended herself so much by judicious and sympathetic assent, that Mrs. Lander learned with a shock of disappointment that her mother expected her to bring the garment home with her, where Mrs. Lander was to come and have it fitted over for the alterations she wanted made.

"But I supposed, from what Mr. Landa said, that your motha would come here and fit me!" she lamented.

"I guess he didn't undastand, 'm. Motha doesn't eva go out to do wo'k," said Clementina gently but firmly.

"Well, I might have known Mr. Landa would mix it up, if it could be mixed;" Mrs. Lander's sense of injury was aggravated by her suspicion that he had brought the girl in the hope of pleasing her, and confirming her in the wish to have her with them; she was not a woman who liked to have her way in spite of herself; she wished at every step to realize that she was taking it, and that no one else was taking it for her.

"Well," she said dryly, "I shall have to see about it. I'm a good deal of an invalid, and I don't know as I could go back and fo'th to try on. I'mmoa used to havin' the things brought to me."

"Yes'm," said Clementina. She moved a little from the bed, on her way to the door, to be ready for Mrs. Lander in leave-taking.

"I'm real sorry," said Mrs. Lander. "I presume it's a disappointment for you, too."

"Oh, not at all," answered Clementina. "I'm sorry we can't do the wo'k he'a; but I know mocha wouldn't like to. Good-mo'ning,'m!"

"No, no! Don't go yet a minute! Won't you just give me my hand bag off the bureau the'a?" Mrs. Lander entreated, and when the girl gave her the bag she felt about among the banknotes which she seemed to have loose in it, and drew out a handful of them without regard to their value. "He'a!" she said, and she tried to put the notes into Clementina's hand, "I want you should get yourself something."

The girl shrank back. "Oh, no'm," she said, with an effect of seeming to know that her refusal would hurt, and with the wish to soften it. "I - couldn't; indeed I couldn't."

"Why couldn't you? Now you must! If I can't let you have the wo'k the way you want, I don't think it's fair, and you ought to have the money for it just the same."

Clementina shook her head smiling. "I don't believe motha would like to have me take it."

"Oh, now, pshaw!" said Mrs. Lander, inadequately. "I want you should take this for youaself; and if you don't want to buy anything to wea', you can get something to fix your room up with. Don't you be afraid of robbin' us. Land! We got moa money! Now you take this."

Mrs. Lander reached the money as far toward Clementina as she could and shook it in the vehemence of her desire.

"Thank you, I couldn't take it," Clementina persisted. "I'm afraid I must be going; I guess I must bid you good-mo'ning."

"Why, I believe the child's sca'ed of me! But you needn't be. Don't you suppose I know how you feel? You set down in that chai'a there, and I'll tell you how you feel. I guess we've been pooa, too - I don't mean anything that a'n't exactly right - and I guess I've had the same feelin's. You think it's demeanin' to you to take it. A'n't that it?" Clementina sank provisionally upon the edge of the chair. "Well, it did use to be so consid'ed. But it's all changed, nowadays. We travel pretty nee' the whole while, Mr. Lander and me, and we see folks everywhere, and it a'n't the custom to refuse any moa. Now, a'n't there any little thing for your own room, there in your nice new house? Or something your motha's got her heat set on? Or one of your brothas? My, if you don't have it, some one else will! Do take it!"

The girl kept slipping toward the door. "I shouldn't know what to tell them, when I got home. They would think I must be - out of my senses."

"I guess you mean they'd think I was. Now, listen to me a minute!" Mrs. Lander persisted.

"You just take this money, and when you get home, you tell your mother every word about it, and if she says, you bring it right straight back to me. Now, can't you do that?"

"I don't know but I can," Clementina faltered. "Well, then take it!" Mrs. Lander put the bills into her hand but she did not release her at once. She pulled Clementina down and herself up till she could lay her other arm on her neck. "I want you should let me kiss you. Will you?"

"Why, certainly," said Clementina, and she kissed the old woman.

"You tell your mother I'm comin' to see her before I go; and I guess," said Mrs. Lander in instant expression of the idea that came into her mind, "we shall be goin' pretty soon, now."

"Yes'm," said Clementina.

She went out, and shortly after Lander came in with a sort of hopeful apathy in his face.

Mrs. Lander turned her head on her pillow, and so confronted him. "Albe't, what made you want me to see that child?"

Lander must have perceived that his wife meant business, and he came to it at once. "I thought you might take a fancy to her, and get her to come and live with us."

"Yes?"

"We're both of us gettin' pretty well on, and you'd ought to have somebody to look after you if - I'm not around. You want somebody that can do for you; and keep you company, and read to you, and talk to you - well, moa like a daughta than a suvvant - somebody that you'd get attached to, maybe - "

"And don't you see," Mrs. Lander broke out severely upon him, "what a ca'e that would be? Why, it's got so already that I can't help thinkin' about her the whole while, and if I got attached to her I'd have her on my mind day and night, and the moa she done for me the more I should be tewin' around to do for her. I shouldn't have any peace of my life any moa. Can't you see that?"

"I guess if you see it, I don't need to," said Lander.

"Well, then, I want you shouldn't eva mention her to me again. I've had the greatest escape! But I've got her off home, and I've give her money enough! had a time with her about it - so that they won't feel as if we'd made 'em trouble for nothing, and now I neva want to hear of her again. I don't want we should stay here a great while longer; I shall be frettin' if I'm in reach of her, and I shan't get any good of the ai'a. Will you promise?"

"Yes."

"Well, then!" Mrs. Lander turned her face upon the pillow again in the dramatization of her exhaustion; but she was not so far gone that she was insensible to the possible interest that a light rap at the door suggested. She once more twisted her head in that direction and called, "Come in!"

The door opened and Clementina came in. She advanced to the bedside smiling joyously, and put the money Mrs. Lander had given her down upon the counterpane.

"Why, you haven't been home, child?"

"No'm," said Clementina, breathlessly. "But I couldn't take it. I knew they wouldn't want me to, and I thought you'd like it better if I just brought it back myself. Good-mo'ning." She slipped out of the door. Mrs. Lander swept the bank-notes from the coverlet and pulled it over her head, and sent from beneath it a stifled wail. "Now we got to go! And it's all youa fault, Albe't."

Lander took the money from the floor, and smoothed each bill out, and then laid them in a neat pile on the corner of the bureau. He sighed profoundly but left the room without an effort to justify himself.

V

The Landers had been gone a week before Clementina's mother decided that she could spare her to Mrs. Atwell for a while. It was established that she was not to serve either in the dining-room or the carving room; she was not to wash dishes or to do any part of the chamber work, but to carry messages and orders for the landlady, and to save her steps, when she wished to see the head-waiter, or the head-cook; or to make an excuse or a promise to some of the lady-boarders; or to send word to Mr. Atwell about the buying, or to communicate with the clerk about rooms taken or left.

She had a good deal of dignity of her own and such a gravity in the discharge of her duties that the chef, who was a middle-aged Yankee with grown girls of his own, liked to pretend that it was Mrs. Atwell herself who was talking with him, and to discover just as she left him that it was Clementina. He called her the Boss when he spoke of her to others in her hearing, and he addressed her as Boss when he feigned to find that it was not Mrs. Atwell. She did not mind that in him, and let the chef have his joke as if it were not one. But one day when the clerk called her Boss she merely looked at him without speaking, and made him feel that he had taken a liberty which he must not repeat. He was a young man who much preferred a state of self-satisfaction to humiliation of any sort, and after he had endured Clementina's gaze as long as he could, he said, "Perhaps you don't allow anybody but the chef to call you that?"

She did not answer, but repeated the message Mrs. Atwell had given her for him, and went away.

It seemed to him undue that a person who exchanged repartees with the young lady boarders across his desk, when they came many times a day to look at the register, or to ask for letters, should remain snubbed by a girl who still wore her hair in a braid; but he was an amiable youth, and he tried to appease her by little favors and services, instead of trying to bully her.

He was great friends with the head-waiter, whom he respected as a college student, though for the time being he ranked the student socially. He had him in behind the frame of letter-boxes, which formed a sort of little private room for him, and talked with him at such hours of the forenoon and the late evening as the student was off duty. He found comfort in the student's fretful strength, which expressed itself in the pugnacious frown of his hot-looking young face, where a bright sorrel mustache was beginning to blaze on a short upper lip.

Fane thought himself a good-looking fellow, and he regarded his figure with pleasure, as it was set off by the suit of fine gray check that he wore habitually; but he thought Gregory's educational advantages told in his face. His own education had ended at a commercial college, where he acquired a good knowledge of bookkeeping, and the fine business hand he wrote, but where it seemed to him sometimes that the earlier learning of the public school had been hermetically sealed within him by several coats of mathematical varnish. He believed that he had once known a number of things that he no longer knew, and that he had not always been so weak in his double letters as he presently found himself.

One night while Gregory sat on a high stool and rested his elbow on the desk before it, with his chin in his hand, looking down upon Fane, who sprawled sadly in his chair, and listening to the last dance playing in the distant parlor, Fane said. "Now, what'll you bet that they won't every one of 'em come and look for a letter in her box before she goes to bed? I tell you, girls are queer, and there's no place like a hotel to study 'em."

"I don't want to study them," said Gregory, harshly.

"Think Greek's more worth your while, or know 'em well enough already?" Fane suggested.

"No, I don't know them at all," said the student.

"I don't believe," urged the clerk, as if it were relevant, "that there's a girl in the house that you couldn't marry, if you gave your mind to it."

Gregory twitched irascibly. "I don't want to marry them."

"Pretty cheap lot, you mean? Well, I don't know."

"I don't mean that," retorted the student. "But I've got other things to think of."

"Don't you believe," the clerk modestly urged, "that it is natural for a man - well, a young man - to think about girls?"

"I suppose it is."

"And you don't consider it wrong?"

"How, wrong?"

"Well, a waste of time. I don't know as I always think about wanting to marry 'em, or be in love, but I like to let my mind run on 'em. There's something about a girl that, well, you don't know what it is, exactly. Take almost any of 'em," said the clerk, with an air of inductive reasoning. "Take that Claxon girl, now for example, I don't know what it is about her. She's good-looking, I don't deny that; and she's got pretty manners, and she's as graceful as a bird. But it a'n't any one of 'em, and it don't seem to be all of 'em put together that makes you want to keep your eyes on her the whole while. Ever noticed what a nice little foot she's got? Or her hands?"

"No," said the student.

"I don't mean that she ever tries to show them off; though I know some girls that would. But she's not that kind. She ain't much more than a child, and yet you got to treat her just like a woman. Noticed the kind of way she's got?"

"No," said the student, with impatience.

The clerk mused with a plaintive air for a moment before he spoke. "Well, it's something as if she'd been trained to it, so that she knew just the right thing to do, every time, and yet I guess it's nature. You know how the chef always calls her the Boss? That explains it about as well as anything, and I presume that's what my mind was running on, the other day, when I called her Boss. But, my! I can't get anywhere near her since!"

"It serves you right," said Gregory. "You had no business to tease her."

"Now, do you think it was teasing? I did, at first, and then again it seemed to me that I came out with the word because it seemed the right one. I presume I couldn't explain that to her."

"It wouldn't be easy."

"I look upon her," said Fane, with an effect of argument in the sweetness of his smile, "just as I would upon any other young lady in the house. Do you spell apology with one p or two?"

"One," said the student, and the clerk made a minute on a piece of paper.

"I feel badly for the girl. I don't want her to think I was teasing her or taking any sort of liberty with her. Now, would you apologize to her, if you was in my place, and would you write a note, or just wait your chance and speak to her?"

Gregory got down from his stool with a disdainful laugh, and went out of the place. "You make me sick, Fane," he said.

The last dance was over, and the young ladies who had been waltzing with one another, came out of the parlor with gay cries and laughter, like summer girls who had been at a brilliant hop, and began to stray down the piazzas, and storm into the office. Several of them fluttered up to the desk, as the clerk had foretold, and looked for letters in the boxes bearing their initials. They called him out, and asked if he had not forgotten something for them. He denied it with a sad, wise smile, and then they tried to provoke him to a belated flirtation, in lack of other material, but he met their overtures discreetly, and they presently said, Well, they guessed they must go; and went. Fane turned to encounter Gregory, who had come in by a side door.

"Fane, I want to beg your pardon. I was rude to you just now."

"Oh, no! Oh, no!" the clerk protested. "That's all right. Sit down a while, can't you, and talk with a fellow. It's early, yet."

"No, I can't. I just wanted to say I was sorry I spoke in that way. Good-night. Is there anything in particular?"

"No; good-night. I was just wondering about - that girl."

"Oh!"

VI

Gregory had an habitual severity with his own behavior which did not stop there, but was always passing on to the behavior of others; and his days went by in alternate offence and reparation to those he had to do with. He had to do chiefly with the dining-room girls, whose susceptibilities were such that they kept about their work bathed in tears or suffused with anger much of the time. He was not only good-looking but he was a college student, and their feelings were ready to bud toward him in tender efflorescence, but he kept them cropped and blighted by his curt words and impatient manner. Some of them loved him for the hurts he did them, and some hated him, but all agreed fondly or furiously that he was too cross for anything. They were mostly young school-mistresses, and whether they were of a soft and amorous make, or of a forbidding temper, they knew enough in spite of their hurts to value a young fellow whose thoughts were not running upon girls all the time. Women, even in their spring-time, like men to treat them as if they had souls as well as hearts, and it was a saving grace in Gregory that he treated them all, the silliest of them, as if they had souls. Very likely they responded more with their hearts than with their souls, but they were aware that this was not his fault.

The girls that waited at table saw that he did not distinguish in manner between them and the girls whom they served. The knot between his brows did not dissolve in the smiling gratitude of the young ladies whom he preceded to their places, and pulled out their chairs for, any more than in the blandishments of a waitress who thanked him for some correction.

They owned when he had been harshest that no one could be kinder if he saw a girl really trying, or more patient with well meaning stupidity, but some things fretted him, and he was as apt to correct a girl in her grammar as in her table service. Out of work hours, if he met any of them, he recognized them with deferential politeness; but he shunned occasions of encounter with them as distinctly as he avoided the ladies among the hotel guests. Some of the table girls pitied his loneliness, and once they proposed that he should read to them on the back piazza in the leisure of their mid-afternoons. He said that he had to keep up with his studies in all the time he could get; he treated their request with grave civility, but they felt his refusal to be final.

He was seen very little about the house outside of his own place and function, and he was scarcely known to consort with anyone but Fane, who celebrated his high sense of the honor to the lady-guests; but if any of these would have been willing to show Gregory that they considered his work to get an education as something that redeemed itself from discredit through the nobility of its object, he gave them no chance to do so.

The afternoon following their talk about Clementina, Gregory looked in for Fane behind the letter boxes, but did not find him, and the girl herself came round from the front to say that he was out buying, but would be back now, very soon; it was occasionally the clerk's business to forage among the farmers for the lighter supplies, such as eggs, and butter, and poultry, and this was the buying that Clementina meant. "Very well, I'll wait here for him a little while," Gregory answered.

"So do," said Clementina, in a formula which she thought polite; but she saw the frown with which Gregory took a Greek book from his pocket, and she hurried round in front of the boxes again, wondering how she could have displeased him. She put her face in sight a moment to explain, "I have got to be here and give out the lettas till Mr. Fane gets back," and then withdrew it. He tried to lose himself in his book, but her tender voice spoke from time to time beyond the boxes, and Gregory kept listening for Clementina to say, "No'm, there a'n't. Perhaps, the'e'll be something the next mail," and "Yes'm, he'e's one, and I guess this paper is for some of youa folks, too."

Gregory shut his book with a sudden bang at last and jumped to his feet, to go away.

The girl came running round the corner of the boxes. "Oh! I thought something had happened."

"No, nothing has happened," said Gregory, with a sort of violence; which was heightened by a sense of the rings and tendrils of loose hair springing from the mass that defined her pretty head. "Don't you know that you oughtn't to say 'No'm' and 'Yes'm?'" he demanded, bitterly, and then he expected to see the water come into her eyes, or the fire into her cheeks.

Clementina merely looked interested. "Did I say that? I meant to say Yes, ma'am and No, ma'am; but I keep forgetting."

"You oughtn't to say anything!" Gregory answered savagely, "Just say Yes, and No, and let your voice do the rest."

"Oh!" said the girl, with the gentlest abeyance, as if charmed with the novelty of the idea. "I should be afraid it wasn't polite."

Gregory took an even brutal tone. It seemed to him as if he were forced to hurt her feelings. But his words, in spite of his tone, were not brutal; they might have even been thought flattering. "The politeness is in the manner, and you don't need anything but your manner."

"Do you think so, truly?" asked the girl joyously. "I should like to try it once!"

He frowned again. "I've no business to criticise your way of speaking."

"Oh yes'm - yes, ma'am; sir, I mean; I mean, Oh, yes, indeed! The'a! It does sound just as well, don't it?" Clementina laughed in triumph at the outcome of her efforts, so that a reluctant visional smile came upon Gregory's face, too. "I'm very mach obliged to you, Mr. Gregory - I shall always want to do it, if it's the right way."

"It's the right way," said Gregory coldly.

"And don't they," she urged, "don't they really say Sir and Ma'am, whe'e - whe'e you came from?"

He said gloomily, "Not ladies and gentlemen. Servants do. Waiters - like me." He inflicted this stab to his pride with savage fortitude and he bore with self-scorn the pursuit of her innocent curiosity.

"But I thought - I thought you was a college student."

"Were," Gregory corrected her, involuntarily, and she said, "Were, I mean."

"I'm a student at college, and here I'm a servant! It's all right!" he said with a suppressed gritting of the teeth; and he added, "My Master was the servant of the meanest, and I must - I beg your pardon for meddling with your manner of speaking -"

"Oh, I'm very much obliged to you; indeed I am. And I shall not care if you tell me of anything that's out of the way in my talking," said Clementina, generously.

"Thank you; I think I won't wait any longer for Mr. Fane."

"Why, I'm su'a he'll be back very soon, now. I'll try not to disturb you any moa."

Gregory turned from taking some steps towards the door, and said, "I wish you would tell Mr. Fane something."

"For you? Why, suttainly!"

"No. For you. Tell him that it's all right about his calling you Boss."

The indignant color came into Clementina's face. "He had no business to call me that."

"No; and he doesn't think he had, now. He's truly sorry for it."

"I'll see," said Clementina.

She had not seen by the time Fane got back. She received his apologies for being gone so long coldly, and went away to Mrs. Atwell, whom she told what had passed between Gregory and herself.

"Is he truly so proud?" she asked.

"He's a very good young man," said Mrs. Atwell, "but I guess he's proud. He can't help it, but you can see he fights against it. If I was you, Clem, I wouldn't say anything to the guls about it."

"Oh, no'm - I mean, no, indeed. I shouldn't think of it. But don't you think that was funny, his bringing in Christ, that way?"

"Well, he's going to be a minister, you know."

"Is he really?" Clementina was a while silent. At last she said, "Don't you think Mr. Gregory has a good many freckles?"

"Well, them red-complected kind is liable to freckle," said Mrs. Atwell, judicially.

After rather a long pause for both of them, Clementina asked, "Do you think it would be nice for me to ask Mr. Gregory about things, when I wasn't suttain?"

"Like what?"

"Oh-wo'ds, and pronunciation; and books to read."

"Why, I presume he'd love to have you. He's always correctin' the guls; I see him take up a book one day, that one of 'em was readin', and when she as't him about it, he said it was rubbage. I guess you couldn't have a betta guide."

"Well, that was what I was thinking. I guess I sha'n't do it, though. I sh'd neva have the courage." Clementina laughed and then fell rather seriously silent again.

VII

One day the shoeman stopped his wagon at the door of the helps' house, and called up at its windows, "Well, guls, any of you want to git a numba foua foot into a rumba two shoe, to-day? Now's youa chance, but you got to be quick abort it. The'e ha'r't but just so many numba two shoes made, and the wohld's full o' rumba foua feet."

The windows filled with laughing faces at the first sound of the shoeman's ironical voice; and at sight of his neat wagon, with its drawers at the rear and sides, and its buggy-hood over the seat where the shoeman lounged lazily holding the reins, the girls flocked down the stairs, and out upon the piazza where the shoe man had handily ranged his vehicle.

They began to ask him if he had not this thing and that, but he said with firmness, "Nothin' but shoes, guls. I did carry a gen'l line, one while, of what you may call ankle-wea', such as spats, and stockin's, and gaitas, but I nova did like to speak of such things befoa ladies, and now I stick ex-elusively to shoes. You know that well enough, guls; what's the use?"

He kept a sober face amidst the giggling that his words aroused, - and let his voice sink into a final note of injury.

"Well, if you don't want any shoes, to-day, I guess I must be goin'." He made a feint of jerking his horse's reins, but forebore at the entreaties that went up from the group of girls.

"Yes, we do!" "Let's see them!" "Oh, don't go!" they chorused in an equally histrionic alarm, and the shoeman got down from his perch to show his wares.

"Now, the'a, ladies," he said, pulling out one of the drawers, and dangling a pair of shoes from it by the string that joined their heels, "the'e's a shoe that looks as good as any Sat'd'y-night shoe you eva see. Looks as han'some as if it had a pasteboa'd sole and was split stock all through, like the kind you buy for a dollar at the store, and kick out in the fust walk you take with your fella - 'r some other gul's fella, I don't ca'e which. And yet that's an honest shoe, made of the best of material all the way through, and in the best manna. Just look at that shoe, ladies; ex-amine it; sha'n't cost you a cent, and I'll pay for youa lost time myself, if any complaint is made." He began to toss pairs of the shoes into the crowd of girls, who caught them from each other before they fell, with hysterical laughter, and ran away with them in-doors to try them on. "This is a shoe that I'm intaducin'," the shoeman went on, "and every pair is warranted - warranted numba two; don't make any otha size, because we want to cata to a strictly numba two custom. If any lady doos feel 'em a little mite too snug, I'm sorry for her, but I can't do anything to help her in this shoe."

"Too snug!" came a gay voice from in-doors. "Why my foot feels puffectly lost in this one."

"All right," the shoeman shouted back. "Call it a numba one shoe and then see if you can't find that lost foot in it, some'eres. Or try a little flour, and see if it won't feel more at home. I've hea'd of a shoe that give that sensation of looseness by not goin' on at all."

The girls exulted joyfully together at the defeat of their companion, but the shoeman kept a grave face, while he searched out other sorts of shoes and slippers, and offered them, or responded to some definite demand with something as near like as he could hope to make serve. The tumult of talk and laughter grew till the chef put his head out of the kitchen door, and then came sauntering across the grass to the helps' piazza. At the same time the clerk suffered himself to be lured from his post by the excitement. He came and stood beside the chef, who listened to the shoeman's flow of banter with a longing to take his chances with him.

"That's a nice hawss," he said. "What'll you take for him?"

"Why, hello!" said the shoeman, with an eye that dwelt upon the chef's official white cap and apron, "You talk English, don't you? Fust off, I didn't know but it was one of them foreign dukes come ova he'a to marry some oua poor millionai'es daughtas." The girls cried out for joy, and the chef bore their mirth stoically, but not without a personal relish of the shoeman's up-and-comingness. "Want a hawss?" asked the shoeman with an air of business. "What'll you give?"

"I'll give you thutty-seven dollas and a half," said the chef.

"Sorry I can't take it. That hawss is sellin' at present for just one hundred and fifty dollars."

"Well," said the chef, "I'll raise you a dolla and a quahta. Say thutty-eight and seventy-five."

"W-ell now, you're gittin' up among the figgas where you're liable to own a hawss. You just keep right on a raisin' me, while I sell these ladies some shoes, and maybe you'll hit it yit, 'fo'e night."

The girls were trying on shoes on every side now, and they had dispensed with the formality of going in-doors for the purpose. More than one put out her foot to the clerk for his opinion of the fit, and the shoeman was mingling with the crowd, testing with his hand, advising from his professional knowledge, suggesting, urging, and in some cases artfully agreeing with the reluctance shown.

"This man," said the chef, indicating Fane, "says you can tell moa lies to the square inch than any man out o' Boston."

"Doos he?" asked the shoeman, turning with a pair of high-heeled bronze slippers in his hand from the wagon. "Well, now, if I stood as nea' tohim as you do, I believe I sh'd hit him."

"Why, man, I can't dispute him!" said the chef, and as if he had now at last scored a point, he threw back his head and laughed. When he brought down his head again, it was to perceive the approach of Clementina. "Hello," he said for her to hear, "he'e comes the Boss. Well, I guess I must be goin'," he added, in mock anxiety. "I'm a goin', Boss, I'm a goin'."

Clementina ignored him. "Mr. Atwell wants to see you a moment, Mr. Fane," she said to the clerk.

"All right, Miss Claxon," Fane answered, with the sorrowful respect which he always showed Clementina, now, "I'll be right there." But he waited a moment, either in expression of his personal independence, or from curiosity to know what the shoeman was going to say of the bronze slippers.

Clementina felt the fascination, too; she thought the slippers were beautiful, and her foot thrilled with a mysterious prescience of its fitness for them.

"Now, the'e, ladies, or as I may say guls, if you'll excuse it in one that's moa like a fatha to you than anything else, in his feelings" - the girls tittered, and some one shouted derisively - "It's true!" - "now there is a shoe, or call it a slippa, that I've rutha hesitated about showin' to you, because I know that you're all rutha serious-minded, I don't ca'e how young ye be, or how good-lookin' ye be; and I don't presume the'e's one among you that's eve' head o' dancin'." In the mirthful hooting and mocking that followed, the shoeman hedged gravely from the extreme position he had taken. "What? Well, maybe you have among some the summa folks, but we all know what summa folks ah', and I don't expect you to patte'n by them. But what I will say is that if any young lady within the sound of my voice," - he looked round for the applause which did not fail him in his parody of the pulpit style - "should get an invitation to a dance next winta, and should feel it a wo'k of a charity to the young man to go, she'll be sorry - on his account, rememba - that she ha'n't got this pair o' slippas.

"The'a! They're a numba two, and they'll fit any lady here, I don't ca'e how small a foot she's got. Don't all speak at once, sistas! Ample time allowed for meals. That's a custom-made shoe, and if it hadn't b'en too small for the lady they was oddid foh, you couldn't-'a' got 'em for less than seven dollas; but now I'm throwin' on 'em away for three."

A groan of dismay went up from the whole circle, and some who had pressed forward for a sight of the slippers, shrank back again.

"Did I hea' just now," asked the shoeman, with a soft insinuation in his voice, and in the glance he suddenly turned upon Clementina, "a party addressed as Boss?" Clementina flushed, but she did not cower; the chef walked away with a laugh, and the shoeman pursued him with his voice. "Not that I am goin' to folla the wicked example of a man who tries tomake spot of young ladies; but if the young lady addressed as Boss -"

"Miss Claxon," said the clerk with ingratiating reverence.

"Miss Claxon - I Stan' corrected," pursued the shoeman. "If Miss Claxon will do me the fava just to try on this slippa, I sh'd be able to tell at the next place I stopped just how it looked on a lady's foot. I see you a'n't any of you disposed to buy 'em this aftanoon, 'and I a'n't complainin'; you done pootty well by me, already, and I don't want to uhge you; but I do want to carry away the picture, in my mind's eye - what you may call a mental photograph - of this slipper on the kind of a foot it was made fob, so't I can praise it truthfully to my next customer. What do you say, ma'am?" he addressed himself with profound respect to Clementina.

"Oh, do let him, Clem!" said one of the girls, and another pleaded, "Just so he needn't tell a story to his next customa," and that made the rest laugh.

Clementina's heart was throbbing, and joyous lights were dancing in her eyes. "I don't care if I do," she said, and she stooped to unlace her shoe, but one of the big girls threw herself on her knees at her feet to prevent her. Clementina remembered too late that there was a hole in her stocking and that her little toe came through it, but she now folded the toe artfully down, and the big girl discovered the hole in time to abet her attempt at concealment. She caught the slipper from the shoeman and harried it on; she tied the ribbons across the instep, and then put on the other. "Now put out youa foot, Clem! Fast dancin' position!" She leaned back upon her own heels, and Clementina daintily lifted the edge of her skirt a little, and peered over at her feet. The slippers might or might not have been of an imperfect taste, in their imitation of the prevalent fashion, but on Clementina's feet they had distinction.

"Them feet was made for them slippas," said the shoeman devoutly.

The clerk was silent; he put his hand helplessly to his mouth, and then dropped it at his side again.

Gregory came round the corner of the building from the dining-room, and the big girl who was crouching before Clementina, and who boasted that she was not afraid of the student, called saucily to him, "Come here, a minute, Mr. Gregory," and as he approached, she tilted aside, to let him see Clementina's slippers.

Clementina beamed up at him with all her happiness in her

eyes, but after a faltering instant, his face reddened through its freckles, and he gave her a rebuking frown and passed on.

"Well, I decla'e!" said the big girl. Fane turned uneasily, and said with a sigh, he guessed he must be going, now.

A blight fell upon the gay spirits of the group, and the shoeman asked with an ironical glance after Gregory's retreating figure, "Owna of this propaty?"

"No, just the ea'th," said the big girl, angrily.

The voice of Clementina made itself heard with a cheerfulness which had apparently suffered no chill, but was really a rising rebellion. "How much ah' the slippas?"

"Three dollas," said the shoeman in a surprise which he could not conceal at Clementina's courage.

She laughed, and stooped to untie the slippers. "That's too much for me."

"Let me untie 'em, Clem," said the big girl. "It's a shame for you eva to take 'em off."

"That's right, lady," said the shoeman. "And you don't eva need to," he added, to Clementina, "unless you object to sleepin' in 'em. You pay me what you want to now, and the rest when I come around the latta paht of August."

"Oh keep 'em, Clem!" the big girl urged, passionately, and the rest joined her with their entreaties.

"I guess I betta not," said Clementina, and she completed the work of taking off the slippers in which the big girl could lend her no further aid, such was her affliction of spirit.

"All right, lady," said the shoeman. "Them's youa slippas, and I'll just keep 'em for you till the latta paht of August."

He drove away, and in the woods which he had to pass through on the road to another hotel he overtook the figure of a man pacing rapidly. He easily recognized Gregory, but he bore him no malice. "Like a lift?" he asked, slowing up beside him.

"No, thank you," said Gregory. "I'm out for the walk." He looked round furtively, and then put his hand on the side of the wagon, mechanically, as if to detain it, while he walked on.

"Did you sell the slippers to the young lady?"

"Well, not as you may say sell, exactly," returned the shoeman, cautiously.

"Have you-got them yet?" asked the student.

"Guess so," said the man. "Like to see 'em?"

He pulled up his horse.

Gregory faltered a moment. Then he said, "I'd like to buy them. Quick!"

He looked guiltily about, while the shoeman alertly obeyed, with some delay for a box to put them in. "How much are they?"

"Well, that's a custom made slipper, and the price to the lady that oddid 'em was seven dollas. But I'll let you have 'em for three - if you want 'em for a present." - The shoeman was far too discreet to permit himself anything so overt as a smile; he merely let a light of intelligence come into his face.

Gregory paid the money. "Please consider this as confidential," he said, and he made swiftly away. Before the shoeman could lock the drawer that had held the slippers, and clamber to his perch under the buggy-hood, Gregory was running back to him again.

"Stop!" he called, and as he came up panting in an excitement which the shoeman might well have mistaken for indignation attending the discovery of some blemish in his purchase. "Do you regard this as in any manner a deception?" he palpitated.

"Why," the shoeman began cautiously, "it wa'n't what you may call a promise, exactly. More of a joke than anything else, I looked on it. I just said I'd keep 'em for her; but - "

"You don't understand. If I seemed to disapprove - if I led any one to suppose, by my manner, or by - anything - that I thought it unwise or unbecoming to buy the shoes, and then bought them myself, do you think it is in the nature of an acted falsehood?"

"Lo'd no!" said the shoeman, and he caught up the slack of his reins to drive on, as if he thought this amusing maniac might also be dangerous.

Gregory stopped him with another question. "And shall - will you - think it necessary to speak of - of this transaction? I leave you free!"

"Well," said the shoeman. "I don't know what you're after, exactly, but if you think I'm so shot on for subjects that I've got to tell the folks at the next stop that I sold a fellar a pair of slippas for his gul - Go 'long!" he called to his horse, and left Gregory standing in the middle of the road.

VIII

The people who came to the Middlemount in July were ordinarily the nicest, but that year the August folks were nicer than usual and there were some students among them, and several graduates just going into business, who chose to take their outing there instead of going to the sea-side or the North Woods. This was a chance that might not happen in years again, and it made the house very gay for the young ladies; they ceased to pay court to the clerk, and asked him for letters only at mail-time. Five or six couples were often on the floor together, at the hops, and the young people sat so thick upon the stairs that one could scarcely get up or down.

So many young men made it gay not only for the young ladies, but also for a certain young married lady, when she managed to shirk her rather filial duties to her husband, who was much about the verandas, purblindly feeling his way with a stick, as he walked up and down, or sitting opaque behind the glasses that preserved what was left of his sight, while his wife read to him. She was soon acquainted with a good many more people than he knew, and was in constant request for such occasions as needed a chaperon not averse to mountain climbing, or drives to other hotels for dancing and supper and return by moonlight, or the more boisterous sorts of charades; no sheet and pillow case party was complete without her; for welsh-rarebits her presence was essential. The event of the conflict between these social claims and her duties to her husband was her appeal to Mrs. Atwell on a point which the landlady referred to Clementina.

"She wants somebody to read to her husband, and I don't believe but what you could do it, Clem. You're a good reader, as good as I want to hear, and while you may say that you don't put in a great deal of elocution, I guess you can read full well enough. All he wants is just something to keep him occupied, and all she wants is a chance to occupy herself with otha folks. Well, she is moa their own age. I d'know as the's any hahm in her. And my foot's so much betta, now, that I don't need you the whole while, any moa."

"Did you speak to her about me?" asked the girl.

"Well, I told her I'd tell you. I couldn't say how you'd like."

"Oh, I guess I should like," said Clementina, with her eyes shining. "But - I should have to ask motha."

"I don't believe but what your motha'd be willin'," said Mrs. Atwell. "You just go down and see her about it."

The next day Mrs. Milray was able to take leave of her husband, in setting off to matronize a coaching party, with an exuberance of good conscience that she shared with the spectators. She kissed him with lively affection, and charged him not to let the child read herself to death for him. She captioned Clementina that Mr. Milray never knew when he was tired, and she had better go by the clock in her reading, and not trust to any sign from him.

Clementina promised, and when the public had followed Mrs. Milray away, to watch her ascent to the topmost seat of the towering coach, by means of the ladder held in place by two porters, and by help of the down-stretched hands of all the young men on the coach, Clementina opened the book at the mark she found in it, and began to read to Mr. Milray.

The book was a metaphysical essay, which he professed to find a lighter sort of reading than fiction; he said most novelists were too seriously employed in preventing the marriage of the lovers, up to a certain point, to be amusing; but you could always trust a metaphysician for entertainment if he was very much in earnest, and most metaphysicians were. He let Clementina read on a good while in her tender voice, which had still so many notes of childhood in it, before he manifested any consciousness of being read to. He kept the smile on his delicate face which had come there when his wife said at parting, "I don't believe I should leave her with you if you could see how prettty she was," and he held his head almost motionlessly at the same poise he had given it in listening to her final charges. It was a fine head, still well covered with soft hair, which lay upon it in little sculpturesque masses, like chiseled silver, and the acquiline profile had a purity of line in the arch of the high nose and the jut of the thin lips and delicate chin, which had not been lost in the change from youth to age. One could never have taken it for the profile of a New York lawyer who had early found New York politics more profitable than law, and after a long time passed in city affairs, had emerged with a name shadowed by certain doubtful transactions. But this was Milray's history, which in the rapid progress of American events, was so far forgotten that you had first to remind people of what he had helped do before you could enjoy their surprise in realizing that this gentle person, with the cast of intellectual refinement which distinguished his face, was the notorious Milray, who was once in all the papers. When he made his game and retired from politics, his family would have sacrificed itself a good deal to reclaim him socially, though they were of a severer social than spiritual conscience, in the decay of some ancestral ideals. But he had rendered their willingness hopeless by marrying, rather late in life, a young girl from the farther West who had come East with a general purpose to get on. She got on very well with Milray, and it was perhaps not altogether her own fault that she did not get on so well with his family, when she began to substitute a society aim for the artistic ambition that had brought her to New York. They might have forgiven him for marrying her, but they could not forgive her for marrying him. They were of New England origin and they were perhaps a little more critical with her than if they had been New Yorkers of Dutch strain. They said that she was a little Western hoyden, but that the stage would have been a good place for her if she could have got over her Pike county accent; in the hush of family councils they confided to one another the belief that there were phases of the variety business in which her accent would have been no barrier to her success, since it could not have been heard in the dance, and might have been disguised in the song.

"Will you kindly read that passage over again?" Milray asked as Clementina paused at the end of a certain paragraph. She read it, while he listened attentively. "Could you tell me just what you understand by that?" he pursued, as if he really expected Clementina to instruct him.

She hesitated a moment before she answered, "I don't believe I undastand anything at all."

"Do you know," said Milray, "that's exactly my own case? And I've an idea that the author is in the same box," and Clementina perceived she might laugh, and laughed discreetly.

Milray seemed to feel the note of discreetness in her laugh, and he asked, smiling, "How old did you tell me you were?"

"I'm sixteen," said Clementina.

"It's a great age," said Milray. "I remember being sixteen myself; I have never been so old since. But I was very old for my age, then. Do you think you are?"

"I don't believe I am," said Clementina, laughing again, but still very discreetly.

"Then I should like to tell you that you have a very agreeable voice. Do you sing?"

"No'm - no, sir - no," said Clementina, "I can't sing at all."

"Ah, that's very interesting," said Milray, "but it's not

surprising. I wish I could see your face distinctly; I've a great curiosity about matching voices and faces; I must get Mrs. Milray to tell me how you look. Where did you pick up your pretty knack at reading? In school, here?"

"I don't know," answered Clementina. "Do I read-the way you want?"

"Oh, perfectly. You let the meaning come through - when there is any."

"Sometimes," said Clementina ingenuously, "I read too fast; the children ah' so impatient when I'm reading to them at home, and they hurry me. But I can read a great deal slower if you want me to."

"No, I'm impatient, too," said Milray. "Are there many of them, - the children?"

"There ah' six in all."

"And are you the oldest?"

"Yes," said Clementina. She still felt it very blunt not to say sir, too, but she tried to make her tone imply the sir, as Mr. Gregory had bidden her.

"You've got a very pretty name."

Clementina brightened. "Do you like it? Motha gave it to me; she took it out of a book that fatha was reading to her."

"I like it very much," said Milray. "Are you tall for your age?"

"I guess I am pretty tall."

"You're fair, of course. I can tell that by your voice; you've got a light-haired voice. And what are your eyes?"

"Blue!" Clementina laughed at his pursuit.

"Ah, of course! It isn't a gray-eyed blonde voice. Do you think - has anybody ever told you-that you were graceful?"

"I don't know as they have," said Clementina, after thinking.

"And what is your own opinion?" Clementina began to feel her dignity infringed; she did not answer, and now Milray laughed. "I felt the little tilt in your step as you came up. It's all right. Shall we try for our friend's meaning, now?"

Clementina began again, and again Milray stopped her. "You mustn't bear malice. I can hear the grudge in your voice; but I didn't mean to laugh at you. You don't like being made fun of, do you?"

"I don't believe anybody does," said Clementina.

"No, indeed," said Milray. "If I had tried such a thing I should be afraid you would make it uncomfortable for me. But I haven't, have I?"

"I don't know," said Clementina, reluctantly.

Milray laughed gleefully. "Well, you'll forgive me, because I'm an old fellow. If I were young, you wouldn't, would you?"

Clementina thought of the clerk; she had certainly never forgiven him. "Shall I read on?" she asked.

"Yes, yes. Read on," he said, respectfully. Once he interrupted her to say that she pronounced admirable, but he would like now and then to differ with her about a word if she did not mind. She answered, Oh no, indeed; she should like it ever so much, if he would tell her when she was wrong. After that he corrected her, and he amused himself by studying forms of respect so delicate that they should not alarm her pride; Clementina reassured him in terms as fine as his own. She did not accept his instructions implicitly; she meant to bring them to the bar of Gregory's knowledge. If he approved of them, then she would submit.

Milray easily possessed himself of the history of her life and of all its circumstances, and he said he would like to meet her father and make the acquaintance of a man whose mind, as Clementina interpreted it to him, he found so original.

He authorized his wife to arrange with Mrs. Atwell for a monopoly of Clementina's time while he stayed at Middlemount, and neither he nor Mrs. Milray seemed surprised at the good round sum, as the landlady thought it, which she asked in the girl's behalf.

IX

The Milrays stayed through August, and Mrs. Milray was the ruling spirit of the great holiday of the summer, at Middlemount. It was this year that the landlords of the central mountain region had decided to compete in a coaching parade, and to rival by their common glory the splendor of the East Side and the West Side parades. The boarding-houses were to take part, as well as the hotels; the farms where only three or four summer folks were received, were to send their mountain-wagons, and all were to be decorated with bunting. An arch draped with flags and covered with flowers spanned the entrance to the main street at Middlemount Centre, and every shop in the village was adorned for the event.

Mrs. Milray made the landlord tell her all about coaching parades, and the champions of former years on the East Side and the West Side, and then she said that the Middlemount House must take the prize from them all this year, or she should never come near his house again. He answered, with a dignity and spirit he rarely showed with Mrs. Milray's class of custom, "I'm goin' to drive our hossis myself."

She gave her whole time to imagining and organizing the personal display on the coach. She consulted with the other ladies as to the kind of dresses that were to be worn, but she decided everything herself; and when the time came she had all the young men ravaging the lanes and pastures for the goldenrod and asters which formed the keynote of her decoration for the coach.

She made peace and kept it between factions that declared themselves early in the affair, and of all who could have criticized her for taking the lead perhaps none would have willingly relieved her of the trouble. She freely declared that it was killing her, and she sounded her accents of despair all over the place. When their dresses were finished she made the persons of her drama rehearse it on the coach top in the secret of the barn, where no one but the stable men were suffered to see the effects she aimed at. But on the eve of realizing these in public she was overwhelmed by disaster. The crowning glory of her composition was to be a young girl standing on the highest seat of the coach, in the character of the Spirit of Summer, wreathed and garlanded with flowers, and invisibly sustained by the twelve months of the year, equally divided as to sex, but with the more difficult and painful attitudes assigned to the gentlemen who were to figure as the fall and winter months. It had been all worked out and the actors drilled in their parts, when the Spirit of Summer, who had been chosen for the inoffensiveness of her extreme youth, was taken with mumps, and withdrawn by the doctor's orders. Mrs. Milray had now not only to improvise another Spirit of Summer, but had to choose her from a group of young ladies, with the chance of alienating and embittering those who were not chosen. In her calamity she asked her husband what she should do, with but the least hope that he could tell her. But he answered promptly, "Take Clementina; I'll let you have her for the day," and then waited for the storm of her renunciations and denunciations to spend itself.

"To be sure," she said, when this had happened, "it isn't as if she were a servant in the house; and the position can be regarded as a kind of public function, anyhow. I can't say that I've hired her to take the part, but I can give her a present afterwards, and it will be the same thing."

The question of clothes for Clementina Mrs. Milray declared was almost as sweeping in its implication as the question of the child's creation. "She has got to be dressed new from head to foot," she said, "every stitch, and how am I to manage it in twenty-four hours?"

By a succession of miracles with cheese-cloth, and sashes and ribbons, it was managed; and ended in a triumph so great that Mrs. Milray took the girl in her arms and kissed her for looking the Spirit of Summer to a perfection that the victim of the mumps could not have approached. The victory was not lastingly marred by the failure of Clementina's shoes to look the Spirit of Summer as well as the rest of her costume. No shoes at all world have been the very thing, but shoes so shabby and worn down at one side of the heel as Clementina's were very far from the thing. Mrs. Milray decided that another fold of cheese-cloth would add to the statuesque charm of her figure, and give her more height; and she was richly satisfied with the effect when the Middlemount coach drove up to the great veranda the next morning, with all the figures of her picture in position on its roof, and Clementina supreme among them. She herself mounted in simple, undramatized authority to her official seat beside the landlord, who in coachman's dress, with a bouquet of autumnal flowers in his lapel, sat holding his garlanded reins over the backs of his six horses; and then the coach as she intended it to appear in the parade set out as soon as the turnouts of the other houses joined it. They were all to meet at the Middlemount, which was thickly draped and festooned in flags, with knots of evergreen and the first red boughs of the young swamp maples holding them in place over its irregular facade. The coach itself was amass of foliage and flowers, from which it defined itself as a wheeled vehicle in vague and partial outline; the other wagons and coaches, as they drove tremulously up, with an effect of having been mired in blossoms about their spokes and hubs, had the unwieldiness which seems inseparable from spectacularity. They represented motives in color and design sometimes tasteless enough, and sometimes so nearly very good that Mrs. Milray's heart was a great deal in her mouth, as they arrived, each with its hotel-cry roared and shrilled from a score of masculine and feminine throats, and finally spelled for distinctness sake, with an ultimate yell or growl. But she had not finished giving the lady-representative of a Sunday newspaper the points of her own tableau, before she regained the courage and the faith in which she remained serenely steadfast throughout the parade.

It was when all the equipages of the neighborhood had arrived that she climbed to her place; the ladder was taken away; the landlord spoke to his horses, and the Middlemount coach led the parade, amid the renewed slogans, and the cries and fluttered handkerchiefs of the guests crowding the verandas.

The line of march was by one road to Middlemount Centre, where the prize was to be awarded at the judges' stand, and then the coaches were to escort the triumphant vehicle homeward by another route, so as to pass as many houses on the way as possible. It was a curious expression of the carnival spirit in a region immemorially starved of beauty in the lives of its people; and whatever was the origin of the mountain coaching parade, or from whatever impulse of sentimentality or advertising it came, the effect was of undeniable splendor, and of phantasmagoric strangeness.

Gregory watched its progress from a hill-side pasture as it trailed slowly along the rising and falling road. The songs of the young girls, interrupted by the explosion of hotel slogans and college cries from the young men, floated off to him on the thin breeze of the cloudless August morning, like the hymns and shouts of a saturnalian rout going in holiday processional to sacrifice to their gods. Words of fierce Hebrew poetry burned in his thought; the warnings and the accusals and the condemnations of the angry prophets; and he stood rapt from his own time and place in a dream of days when the Most High stooped to commune face to face with His ministers, while the young voices of those forgetful or ignorant of Him, called to his own youth, and the garlanded chariots, with their banners and their streamers passed on the road beneath him and out of sight in the shadow of the woods beyond.

When the prize was given to the Middlemount coach at the

Center the landlord took the flag, and gallantly transferred it to Mrs. Milray, and Mrs. Milray passed it up to Clementina, and bade her, "Wave it, wave it!"

The village street was thronged with people that cheered, and swung their hats and handkerchiefs to the coach as it left the judges' stand and drove under the triumphal arch, with the other coaches behind it. Then Atwell turned his horses heads homewards, and at the brisker pace with which people always return from festivals or from funerals, he left the village and struck out upon the country road with his long escort before him. The crowd was quick to catch the courteous intention of the victors, and followed them with applause as far beyond the village borders as wind and limb would allow; but the last noisy boy had dropped off breathless before they reached a half-finished house in the edge of some woods. A line of little children was drawn up by the road-side before it, who watched the retinue with grave eagerness, till the Middlemount coach came in full sight. Then they sprang into the air, and beating their hands together, screamed, "Clem! Clem! Oh it's Clem!" and jumped up and down, and a shabby looking work worn woman came round the corner of the house and stared up at Clementina waving her banner wildly to the children, and shouting unintelligible words to them. The young people on the coach joined in response to the children, some simply, some ironically, and one of the men caught up a great wreath of flowers which lay at Clementina's feet, and flung it down to them; the shabby woman quickly vanished round the corner of the house again. Mrs. Milray leaned over to ask the landlord, "Who in the world are Clementina's friends?"

"Why don't you know?" he retorted in abated voice. "Them's her brothas and sistas."

"And that woman?"

"The lady at the conna? That's her motha."

When the event was over, and all the things had been said and said again, and there was nothing more to keep the spring and summer months from going up to their rooms to lie down, and the fall and winter months from trying to get something to eat, Mrs. Milray found herself alone with Clementina.

The child seemed anxious about something, and Mrs. Milray, who wanted to go and lie down, too, asked a little impatiently, "What is it, Clementina?"

"Oh, nothing. Only I was afraid maybe you didn't like my waving to the children, when you saw how queea they looked." Clementina's lips quivered.

"Did any of the rest say anything?"

"I know what they thought. But I don't care! I should do it right over again!"

Mrs. Milray's happiness in the day's triumph was so great that she could indulge a generous emotion. She caught the girl in her arms. "I want to kiss you; I want to hug you, Clementina!"

The notion of a dance for the following night to celebrate the success of the house in the coaching parade came to Mrs. Milray aver a welsh-rarebit which she gave at the close of the evening. The party was in the charge of Gregory, who silently served them at their orgy with an austerity that might have conspired with the viand itself against their dreams, if they had not been so used to the gloom of his ministrations. He would not allow the waitresses to be disturbed in their evening leisure, or kept from their sleep by such belated pleasures; and when he had provided the materials for the rarebit, he stood aloof, and left their combination to Mrs. Milray and her chafing-dish.

She had excluded Clementina on account of her youth, as she said to one of the fall and winter months, who came in late, and noticed Clementina's absence with a "Hello! Anything the matter with the Spirit of Summer?" Clementina had become both a pet and a joke with these months before the parade was over, and now they clamored together, and said they must have her at the dance anyway. They were more tepidly seconded by the spring and summer months, and Mrs. Milray said, "Well, then, you'll have to all subscribe and get her a pair of dancing slippers." They pressed her for her meaning, and she had to explain the fact of Clementina's destitution, which that additional fold of cheese-cloth had hidden so well in the coaching tableau that it had never been suspected. The young men entreated her to let them each buy a pair of slippers for the Spirit of Summer, which she should wear in turn for the dance that she must give each of them; and this made Mrs. Milray declare that, no, the child should not come to the dance at all, and that she was not going to have her spoiled. But, before the party broke up, she promised that she would see what could be done, and she put it very prettily to the child the next day, and waited for her to say, as she knew she must, that she could not go, and why. They agreed that the cheese-cloth draperies of the Spirit of Summer were surpassingly fit for the dance; but they had to agree that this still left the question of slippers untouched. It remained even more hopeless when Clementina tried on all of Mrs. Milray's festive shoes, and none of her razorpoints and high heels would avail. She went away disappointed, but not yet disheartened; youth does not so easily renounce a pleasure pressed to the lips; and Clementina had it in her head to ask some of the table girls to help her out. She meant to try first with that big girl who had helped her put on the shoeman's bronze slippers; and she hurried through the office, pushing purblindly past Fane without looking his way, when he called to her in the deference which he now always used with her, "Here's a package here for you, Clementina - Miss Claxon," and he gave her an oblong parcel, addressed in a hand strange to her. "Who is it from?" she asked, innocently, and Fane replied with the same ingenuousness: "I'm sure I don't know." Afterwards he thought of having retorted, "I haven't opened it," but still without being certain that he would have had the courage to say it.

Clementina did not think of opening it herself, even when she was alone in her little room above Mrs. Atwell's, until she had carefully felt it over, and ascertained that it was a box of pasteboard, three or four inches deep and wide, and eight or ten inches long. She looked at the address again, "Miss Clementina Claxon," and at the narrow notched ribbon which tied it, and noted that the paper it was wrapped in was very white and clean. Then she sighed, and loosed the knot, and the paper slipped off the box, and at the same time the lid fell off, and the shoe man's bronze slippers fell out upon the floor.

Either it must be a dream or it must be a joke; it could not be both real and earnest; somebody was trying to tease her; such flattery of fortune could not be honestly meant. But it went to her head, and she was so giddy with it as she caught the slippers from the floor, and ran down to Mrs. Atwell, that she knocked against the sides of the narrow staircase.

"What is it? What does it mean? Who did it?" she panted, with the slippers in her hand. "Whe'e did they come from?" She poured out the history of her trying on these shoes, and of her present need of them and of their mysterious coming, to meet her longing after it had almost ceased to be a hope. Mrs. Atwell closed with her in an exultation hardly short of a clapping the hands. Her hair was gray, and the girl's hair still hung in braids down her back, but they were of the same age in their transport, which they referred to Mrs. Milray, and joined with her in glad but fruitless wonder who had sent Clementina the shoes. Mrs. Atwell held that the help who had seen the girl trying them on had clubbed together and got them for her at the time; and had now given them to her for the honor she had done the Middlemount House in the parade. Mrs. Milray argued that the spring and summer months had secretly dispatched some fall and winter month to ransack the stores at Middlemount Centre for them. Clementina believed that they came from the shoe man himself, who had always wanted to send them, in the hope that she would keep them, and had merely happened to send them just then in that moment of extremity when she was helpless against them. Each conjecture involved improbabilities so gross that it left the field free to any opposite theory.

Rumor of the fact could not fail to go through the house, and long before his day's work was done it reached the chef, and amused him as a piece of the Boss's luck. He was smoking his evening pipe at the kitchen door after supper, when Clementina passed him on one of the many errands that took her between Mrs. Milray's room and her own, and he called to her: "Boss, what's this I hear about a pair o' glass slippas droppin' out the sky int' youa lap?"

Clementina was so happy that she thought she might trust him for once, and she said, "Oh, yes, Mr. Mahtin! Who do you suppose sent them?" she entreated him so sweetly that it would have softened any heart but the heart of a tease.

"I believe I could give a pootty good guess if I had the facts."

Clementina innocently gave them to him, and he listened with a well-affected sympathy.

"Say Fane fust told you about 'em?"

"Yes. 'He'e's a package for you,' he said. Just that way; and he couldn't tell me who left it, or anything."

"Anybody asked him about it since?"

"Oh, yes! Mrs. Milray, and Mrs. Atwell, and Mr. Atwell, and everybody."

"Everybody." The chef smiled with a peculiar droop of one eye. "And he didn't know when the slippas got into the landlo'd's box?"

"No. The fust thing he knew, the' they we'e!" Clementina stood expectant, but the chef smoked on as if that were all there was to say, and seemed to have forgotten her. "Who do you think put them thea, Mr. Mahtin?"

The chef looked up as if surprised to find her still there. "Oh! Oh, yes! Who d' I think? Why, I know, Boss. But I don't believe I'd betta tell you."

"Oh, do, Mr. Mahtin! If you knew how I felt about it -"

"No, no! I guess I betta not. 'Twouldn't do you any good. I guess I won't say anything moa. But if I was in youa place, and I really wanted to know whe'e them slippas come from -"

"I do - I do indeed -"

The chef paused before he added, "I should go at Fane. I guess what he don't know ain't wo'th knowin', and I guess nobody else knows anything. Thea! I don't know but I said mo'n I ought, now."

What the chef said was of a piece with what had been more than once in Clementina's mind; but she had driven it out, not because it might not be true, but because she would not have it true. Her head drooped; she turned limp and springless away. Even the heart of the tease was touched; he had not known that it would worry her so much, though he knew that she disliked the clerk.

"Mind," he called after her, too late, "I ain't got no proof 't he done it."

She did not answer him, or look round. She went to her room, and sat down in the growing dusk to think, with a hot lump in her throat.

Mrs. Atwell found her there an hour later, when she climbed to the chamber where she thought she ought to have heard Clementina moving about over her own room.

"Didn't know but I could help you do youa dressin'," she began, and then at sight of the dim figure she broke off: "Why, Clem! What's the matte? Ah' you asleep? Ah' you sick? It's half an hour of the time and -"

"I'm not going," Clementina answered, and she did not move.

"Not goin'! Why the land o' -"

"Oh, I can't go, Mrs. Atwell. Don't ask me! Tell Mrs. Milray, please!"

"I will, when I got something to tell," said Mrs. Atwell. "Now, you just say what's happened, Clementina Claxon!" Clementina suffered the woful truth to be drawn from her. "But you don't know whether it's so or not," the landlady protested.

"Yes, yes, I do! It was the last thing I thought of, and the chef wouldn't have said it if he didn't believe it."

"That's just what he would done," cried Mrs. Atwell. "And I'll give him such a goin' ova, for his teasin', as he ain't had in one while. He just said it to tease. What you goin' to say to Mrs. Milray?"

"Oh, tell her I'm not a bit well, Mrs. Atwell! My head does ache, truly."

"Why, listen," said Mrs. Atwell, recklessly. "If you believe he done it - and he no business to - why don't you just go to the dance, in 'em, and then give 'em back to him after it's ova? It would suv him right."

Clementina listened for a moment of temptation, and then shook her head. "It wouldn't do, Mrs. Atwell; you know it wouldn't," she said, and Mrs. Atwell had too little faith in her suggestion to make it prevail. She went away to carry Clementina's message to Mrs. Milray, and her task was greatly eased by the increasing difficulty Mrs. Milray had begun to find, since the way was perfectly smoothed for her, in imagining the management of Clementina at the dance: neither child nor woman, neither servant nor lady, how was she to be carried successfully through it, without sorrow to herself or offence to others? In proportion to the relief she felt, Mrs. Milray protested her irreconcilable grief; but when the simpler Mrs. Atwell proposed her going and reasoning with Clementina, she said, No, no; better let her alone, if she felt as she did; and perhaps after all she was right.

X

Clementina listened to the music of the dance, till the last note was played; and she heard the gay shouts and laughter of the dancers as they issued from the ball room and began to disperse about the halls and verandas, and presently to call good night to one another. Then she lighted her lamp, and put the slippers back into the box and wrapped it up in the nice paper it had come in, and tied it with the notched ribbon. She thought how she had meant to put the slippers away so, after the dance, when she had danced her fill in them, and how differently she was doing it all now. She wrote the clerk's name on the parcel, and then she took the box, and descended to the office with it. There seemed to be nobody there, but at the noise of her step Fane came round the case of letter-boxes, and advanced to meet her at the long desk.

"What's wanted, Miss Claxon?" he asked, with his hopeless respectfulness. "Anything I can do for you?"

She did not answer, but looked him solemnly in the eyes and laid the parcel down on the open register, and then went out.

He looked at the address on the parcel, and when he untied it, the box fell open and the shoes fell out of it, as they had with Clementina. He ran with them behind the letter-box frame, and held them up before Gregory, who was seated there on the stool he usually occupied, gloomily nursing his knee.

"What do you suppose this means, Frank?"

Gregory looked at the shoes frowningly. "They're the slippers she got to-day. She thinks you sent them to her."

"And she wouldn't have them because she thought I sent them! As sure as I'm standing here, I never did it," said the clerk, solemnly.

"I know it," said Gregory. "I sent them."

"You!"

"What's so wonderful?" Gregory retorted. "I saw that she wanted them that day when the shoe peddler was here. I could see it, and you could."

"Yes."

"I went across into the woods, and the man overtook me with his wagon. I was tempted, and I bought the slippers of him. I wanted to give them to her then, but I resisted, and I thought I should never give them. To-day, when I heard that she was going to that dance, I sent them to her anonymously. That's all there is about it."

The clerk had a moment of bitterness. "If she'd known it was you, she wouldn't have given them back."

"That's to be seen. I shall tell her, now. I never meant her to know, but she must, because she's doing you wrong in her ignorance."

Gregory was silent, and Fane was trying to measure the extent of his own suffering, and to get the whole bearing of the incident in his mind. In the end his attempt was a failure. He asked Gregory, "And do you think you've done just right by me?"

"I've done right by nobody," said Gregory, "not even by myself; and I can see that it was my own pleasure I had in mind. I must tell her the truth, and then I must leave this place."

"I suppose you want I should keep it quiet," said Fane.

"I don't ask anything of you."

"And she wouldn't," said Fane, after reflection. "But I know she'd be glad of it, and I sha'n't say anything. Of course, she never can care for me; and - there's my hand with my word, if you want it." Gregory silently took the hand stretched toward him and Fane added: "All I'll ask is that you'll tell her I wouldn't have presumed to send her the shoes. She wouldn't be mad at you for it."

Gregory took the box, and after some efforts to speak, he went away. It was an old trouble, an old error, an old folly; he had yielded to impulse at every step, and at every step he had sinned against another or against himself. What pain he had now given the simple soul of Fane; what pain he had given that poor child who had so mistaken and punished the simple soul! With Fane it was over now, but with Clementina the worst was perhaps to come yet. He could not hope to see the girl before morning, and then, what should he say to her? At sight of a lamp burning in Mrs. Atwell's room, which was on a level with the veranda where he was walking, it came to him that first of all he ought to go to her, and confess the whole affair; if her husband were with her, he ought to confess before him; they were there in the place of the child's father and mother, and it was due to them. As he pressed rapidly toward the light he framed in his thought the things he should say, and he did not notice, as he turned to enter the private hallway leading to Mrs. Atwell's apartment, a figure at the door. It shrank back from his contact, and he recognized Clementina. His purpose instantly changed, and he said, "Is that you, Miss Claxon? I want to speak with you. Will you come a moment where I can?"

"I - I don't know as I'd betta," she faltered. But she saw the box under his arm, and she thought that he wished to speak to her about that, and she wanted to hear what he would say. She had been waiting at the door there, because she could not bear to go to her room without having something more happen.

"You needn't be afraid. I shall not keep you. Come with me a moment. There is something I must tell you at once. You have made a mistake. And it is my fault. Come!"

Clementina stepped out into the moonlight with him, and they walked across the grass that sloped between the hotel and the river. There were still people about, late smokers singly, and in groups along the piazzas, and young couples, like themselves, strolling in the dry air, under the pure sky.

Gregory made several failures in trying to begin, before he said: "I have to tell you that you are mistaken about Mr. Fane. I was there behind the letter boxes when you came in, and I know that you left these shoes because you thought he sent them to you. He didn't send them." Clementina did not say anything, and Gregory was forced to ask: "Do you wish to know who sent them? I won't tell you unless you do wish it."

"I think I ought to know," she said, and she asked, "Don't you?"

"Yes; for you must blame some one else now, for what you thought Fane did. I sent them to you."

Clementina's heart gave a leap in her breast, and she could not say anything. He went on.

"I saw that you wanted them that day, and when the peddler happened to overtake me in the woods where I was walking, after I left you, I acted on a sudden impulse, and I bought them for you. I meant to send them to you anonymously, then. I had committed one error in acting upon impulse-my rashness is my besetting sin - and I wished to add a species of deceit to that. But I was kept from it until-to-day. I hoped you would like to wear them to the dance to-night, and I put them in the post-office for you myself. Mr. Fane didn't know anything about it. That is all. I am to blame, and no one else."

He waited for her to speak, but Clementina could only say, "I don't know what to say."

"You can't say anything that would be punishment enough for me. I have acted foolishly, cruelly."

Clementina did not think so. She was not indignant, as she was when she thought Fane had taken this liberty with her, but if Mr. Gregory thought it was so very bad, it must be something much more serious than she had imagined. She said, "I don't see why you wanted to do it," hoping that he would be able to tell her something that would make his behavior seem less dreadful than he appeared to think it was.

"There is only one thing that could justify it, and that is something that I cannot justify." It was very mysterious, but youth loves mystery, and Clementina was very young. "I did it," said Gregory solemnly, and he felt that now he was acting from no impulse, but from a wisely considered decision which he might not fail in without culpability, "because I love you."

"Oh!" said Clementina, and she started away from him.

"I knew that it would make me detestable!" he cried, bitterly. "I had to tell you, to explain what I did. I couldn't help doing it. But now if you can forget it, and never think of me again, I can go away, and try to atone for it somehow. I shall be guided."

Clementina did not know why she ought to feel affronted or injured by what he had said to her; but if Mr. Gregory thought it was wrong for him to have spoken so, it must be wrong. She did not wish him to feel badly, even if he had done wrong, but she had to take his view of what he had done. "Why, suttainly, Mr. Gregory," she answered. "You mustn't mind it."

"But I do mind it. I have been very, very selfish, very thoughtless. We are both too young. I can't ask you to wait for me till I could marry -"

The word really frightened Clementina. She said, "I don't believe I betta promise."

"Oh, I know it!" said Gregory. "I am going away from here. I am going to-morrow as soon as I can arrange - as soon as I can get away. Good-night - I" - Clementina in her agitation put her hands up to her face. "Oh, don't cry - I can't bear to have you cry."

She took down her hands. "I'm not crying! But I wish I had neva seen those slippas."

They had come to the bank of the river, whose current quivered at that point in a scaly ripple in the moonlight. At her words Gregory suddenly pulled the box from under his arm, and flung it into the stream as far as he could. It caught upon a shallow of the ripple, hung there a moment, then loosed itself, and swam swiftly down the stream.

"Oh!" Clementina moaned.

"Do you want them back?" he demanded. "I will go in for them!"

"No, no! No. But it seemed such a - waste!"

"Yes, that is a sin, too." They climbed silently to the hotel. At Mrs. Atwell's door, he spoke. "Try to forget what I said, and forgive me, if you can."

"Yes - yes, I will, Mr. Gregory. You mustn't think of it any moa."

XI

Clementina did not sleep till well toward morning, and she was still sleeping when Mrs. Atwell knocked and called in to her that her brother Jim wanted to see her. She hurried down, and in the confusion of mind left over from the night before she cooed sweetly at Jim as if he had been Mr. Gregory, "What is it, Jim? What do you want me for?"

The boy answered with the disgust a sister's company manners always rouse in a brother. "Motha wants you. Says she's wo'ked down, and she wants you to come and help." Then he went his way.

Mrs. Atwell was used to having help snatched from her by their families at a moment's notice. "I presume you've got to go, Clem," she said.

"Oh, yes, I've got to go," Clementina assented, with a note of relief which mystified Mrs. Atwell.

"You tied readin' to Mr. Milray?"

"Oh, no'm-no, I mean. But I guess I betta go home. I guess I've been away long enough."

"Well, you're a good gul, Clem. I presume your motha's got a right to have you home if she wants you." Clementina said nothing to this, but turned briskly, and started upstairs toward her room again. The landlady called after her, "Shall you speak to Mis' Milray, or do you want I should?"

Clementina looked back at her over her shoulder to warble, "Why, if you would, Mrs. Atwell," and kept on to her room.

Mrs. Milray was not wholly sorry to have her go; she was going herself very soon, and Clementina's earlier departure simplified the question of getting rid of her; but she overwhelmed her with reproaches which Clementina received with such sweet sincerity that another than Mrs. Milray might have blamed herself for having abused her ingenuousness.

The Atwells could very well have let the girl walk home, but they sent her in a buckboard, with one of the stablemen to drive her. The landlord put her neat bundle under the seat of the buckboard with his own hand. There was something in the child's bearing, her dignity and her amiability, which made people offer her, half in fun, and half in earnest, the deference paid to age and state.

She did not know whether Gregory would try to see her before she went. She thought he must have known she was going, but since he neither came to take leave of her, nor sent her any message, she decided that she had not expected him to do so. About the third week of September she heard that he had left Middlemount and gone back to college.

She kept at her work in the house and helped her mother, and looked after the little ones; she followed her father in the woods, in his quest of stuff for walking sticks, and advised with both concerning the taste of summer folks in dress and in canes. The winter came, and she read many books in its long leisure, mostly novels, out of the rector's library. He had a whole set of Miss Edgeworth, and nearly all of Miss Austen and Miss Gurney, and he gave of them to Clementina, as the best thing for her mind as well as her morals; he believed nothing could be better for any one than these old English novels, which he had nearly forgotten in their details. She colored the faded English life of the stories afresh from her

Yankee circumstance; and it seemed the consensus of their testimony that she had really been made love to, and not so very much too soon, at her age of sixteen, for most of their heroines were not much older. The terms of Gregory's declaration and of its withdrawal were mystifying, but not more mystifying than many such things, and from what happened in the novels she read, the affair might be trusted to come out all right of itself in time. She was rather thoughtfuller for it, and once her mother asked her what was the matter with her. "Oh, I guess I'm getting old, motha," she said, and turned the question off. She would not have minded telling her mother about Gregory, but it would not have been the custom; and her mother would have worried, and would have blamed him. Clementina could have more easily trusted her father with the case, but so far as she knew fathers never were trusted with anything of the kind. She would have been willing that accident should bring it to the knowledge of Mrs. Richling; but the moment never came when she could voluntarily confide in her, though she was a great deal with her that winter. She was Mrs. Richling's lieutenant in the social affairs of the parish, which the rector's wife took under her care. She helped her get up entertainments of the kind that could be given in the church parlor, and they managed together some dances which had to be exiled to the town hall. They contrived to make the young people of the village feel that they were having a gay time, and Clementina did not herself feel that it was a dull one. She taught them some of the new steps and figures which the help used to pick up from the summer folks at the Middlemount, and practise together; she liked doing that; her mother said the child would rather dance than eat, any time. She was never sad, but so much dignity got into her sweetness that the rector now and then complained of feeling put down by her.

She did not know whether she expected Gregory to write to her or not; but when no letters came she decided that she had not expected them. She wondered if he would come back to the Middlemount the next summer; but when the summer came, she heard that they had another student in his place. She heard that they had a new clerk, and that the boarders were not so pleasant. Another year passed, and towards the end of the season Mrs. Atwell wished her to come and help her again, and Clementina went over to the hotel to soften her refusal. She explained that her mother had so much sewing now that she could not spare her; and Mrs. Atwell said: Well, that was right, and that she must be the greatest kind of dependence for her mother. "You ah' going on seventeen this year, ain't you?"

"I was nineteen the last day of August," said Clementina, and Mrs. Atwell sighed, and said, How the time did fly.

It was the second week of September, but Mrs. Atwell said they were going to keep the house open till the middle of October, if they could, for the autumnal foliage, which there was getting to be quite a class of custom for.

"I presume you knew Mr. Landa was dead," she added, and at Clementina's look of astonishment, she said with a natural satisfaction, "Mm! died the thutteenth day of August. I presumed somehow you'd know it, though you didn't see a great deal of 'em, come to think of it. I guess he was a good man; too good for her, I guess," she concluded, in the New England necessity of blaming some one. "She sent us the papah."

There was an early frost; and people said there was going to be a hard winter, but it was not this that made Clementina's father set to work finishing his house. His turning business was well started, now, and he had got together money enough to pay for the work. He had lately enlarged the scope of his industry by turning gate-posts and urns for the tops of them, which had become very popular, for the front yards of the farm and village houses in a wide stretch of country. They sold more steadily than the smaller wares, the cups, and tops, and little vases and platters which had once been the output of his lathe; after the first season the interest of the summer folks in these fell off; but the gate posts and the urns appealed to a lasting taste in the natives.

Claxon wished to put the finishing touches on the house himself, and he was willing to suspend more profitable labors to do so. After some attempts at plastering he was forced to leave that to the plasterers, but he managed the clap-boarding, with Clementina to hand him boards and nails, and to keep him supplied with the hammer he was apt to drop at critical moments. They talked pretty constantly at their labors, and in their leisure, which they spent on the brown needles under the pines at the side of the house. Sometimes the hammering or the talking would be interrupted by a voice calling, from a passing vehicle in the hidden roadway, something about urns. Claxon would answer, without troubling himself to verify the inquirer; or moving from his place, that he would get round to them, and then would hammer on, or talk on with Clementina.

One day in October a carriage drove up to the door, after the work on the house had been carried as far as Claxon's mood and money allowed, and he and Clementina were picking up the litter of his carpentering. He had replaced the block of wood which once served at the front door by some steps under an arbor of rustic work; but this was still so novel that the younger children had not outgrown their pride in it and were playing at house-keeping there. Clementina ran around to the back door and out through the front entry in time to save the visitor and the children from the misunderstanding they began to fall into, and met her with a smile of hospitable brilliancy, and a recognition full of compassionate welcome.

Mrs. Lander gave way to her tears as she broke out, "Oh, it ain't the way it was the last time I was he'a! You hea'd that he - that Mr. Landa -"

"Mrs. Atwell told me," said Clementina. "Won't you come in, and sit down?"

"Why, yes." Mrs. Lander pushed in through the narrow door of what was to be the parlor. Her crapes swept about her and exhaled a strong scent of their dyes. Her veil softened her heavy face; but she had not grown thinner in her bereavement.

"I just got to the Middlemount last night," she said, "and I wanted to see you and your payrents, both, Miss Claxon. It doos bring him back so! You won't neva know how much he thought of you, and you'll all think I'm crazy. I wouldn't come as long as he was with me, and now I have to come without him; I held out ag'inst him as long as I had him to hold out ag'inst. Not that he was eva one to push, and I don't know as he so much as spoke of it, afta we left the hotel two yea's ago; but I presume it wa'n't out of his mind a single minute. Time and time again I'd say to him, 'Now, Albe't, do you feel about it just the way you done?' and he'd say, 'I ha'r't had any call to charge my mind about it,' and then I'd begin tryin' to ahgue him out of it, and keep a hectorin', till he'd say, 'Well, I'm not askin' you to do it,' and that's all I could get out of him. But I see all the while 't he wanted me to do it, whateva he asked, and now I've got to do it when it can't give him any pleasure." Mrs. Lander put up her black-bordered handkerchief and sobbed into it, and Clementina waited till her grief had spent itself; then she gave her a fan, and Mrs. Lander gratefully cooled her hot wet face. The children had found the noises of her affliction and the turbid tones of her monologue annoying, and had gone off to play in the woods; Claxon kept incuriously about the work that Clementina had left him to; his wife maintained the confidence which she always felt in Clementina's ability to treat with the world when it presented itself, and though she was curious enough, she did not offer to interrupt the girl's interview with Mrs. Lander; Clementina would know how to behave.

Mrs. Lander, when she had refreshed herself with the fan, seemed to get a fresh grip of her theme, and she told Clementina all abort Mr. Lander's last sickness. It had been so short that it gave her no time to try the climate of Colorado upon him, which she now felt sure would have brought him right up; and she had remembered, when too late, to give him a liver-medicine of her own, though it did not appear that it was his liver which was affected; that was the strange part of it.

But, brief as his sickness was, he had felt that it was to be his last, and had solemnly talked over her future with her, which he seemed to think would be lonely. He had not named Clementina, but Mrs. Lander had known well enough what he meant; and now she wished to ask her, and her father and mother, how they would all like Clementina to come and spend the winter with her at Boston first, and then further South, and wherever she should happen to go. She apologized for not having come sooner upon this errand; she had resolved upon it as soon as Mr. Lander was gone, but she had been sick herself, and had only just now got out of bed.

Clementina was too young to feel the pathos of the case fully, or perhaps even to follow the tortuous course of Mrs. Lander's motives, but she was moved by her grief; and she could not help a thrill of pleasure in the vague splendor of the future outlined by Mrs. Lander's proposal. For a time she had thought that Mrs. Milray was going to ask her to visit her in New York; Mrs. Milray had thrown out a hint of something of the kind at parting, but that was the last of it; and now she at once made up her mind that she would like to go with Mrs. Lander, while discreetly saying that she would ask her father and mother to come and talk with her.

XII

Her parents objected to leaving their work; each suggested that the other had better go; but they both came at Clementina's urgence. Her father laughed and her mother frowned when she told them what Mrs. Lander wanted, from the same misgiving of her sanity. They partly abandoned this theory for a conviction of Mrs. Lander's mere folly when she began to talk, and this slowly yielded to the perception that she had some streaks of sense. It was sense in the first place to want to have Clementina with her, and though it might not be sense to suppose that they would be anxious to let her go, they did not find so much want of it as Mrs. Lander talked on. It was one of her necessities to talk away her emotions before arriving at her ideas, which were often found in a tangle, but were not without a certain propriety. She was now, after her interview with Clementina, in the immediate presence of these, and it was her ideas that she began to produce for the girl's father and mother. She said, frankly, that she had more money than she knew what to do with, and they must not think she supposed she was doing a favor, for she was really asking one.

She was alone in the world, without near connections of her own, or relatives of her husband's, and it would be a mercy if they could let their daughter come and visit her; she would not call it more than a visit; that would be the best thing on both sides; she told of her great fancy for Clementina the first time she saw her, and of her husband's wish that she would come and visit with them then for the winter. As for that money she had tried to make the child take, she presumed that they knew about it, and she wished to say that she did it because she was afraid Mr. Lander had said so much about the sewing, that they would be disappointed. She gave way to her tears at the recollection, and confessed that she wanted the child to have the money anyway. She ended by asking Mrs. Claxon if she would please to let her have a drink of water; and she looked about the room, and said that they had got it finished up a great deal, now, had not they? She made other remarks upon it, so apt that Mrs. Claxon gave her a sort of permissive invitation to look about the whole lower floor, ending with the kitchen.

Mrs. Lander sat down there while Mrs. Claxon drew from the pipes a glass of water, which she proudly explained was pumped all over the house by the wind mill that supplied the power for her husband's turning lathes.

"Well, I wish mah husband could have tasted that wata," said Mrs. Lander, as if reminded of husbands by the word, and by the action of putting down the glass. "He was always such a great hand for good, cold wata. My! He'd 'a liked youa kitchen, Mrs. Claxon. He always was such a home-body, and he did get so ti'ed of hotels. For all he had such an appearance, when you see him, of bein' - well! - stiff and proud, he was fah moa common in his tastes - I don't mean common, exactly, eitha - than what I was; and many a time when we'd be drivin' through the country, and we'd pass some o' them long-strung-out houses, don't you know, with the kitchen next to the wood shed, and then an ahchway befoa you get to the stable, Mr. Landa he'd get out, and make an urrand, just so's to look in at the kitchen dooa; he said it made him think of his own motha's kitchen. We was both brought up in the country, that's a fact, and I guess if the truth was known we both expected to settle down and die thea, some time; but now he's gone, and I don't know what'll become o' me, and sometimes I don't much care. I guess if Mr. Landa'd 'a seen youa kitchen, it wouldn't 'a' been so easy to git him out of it; and I do believe if he's livin' anywhe' now he takes as much comfo't in my settin' here as what I do. I presume I shall settle down somewhe's before a great while, and if you could make up youa mind to let your daughta come to me for a little visit till spring, you couldn't do a thing that 'd please Mr. Landa moa."

Mrs. Claxon said that she would talk it over with the child's father; and then Mrs. Lander pressed her to let her take Clementina back to the Middlemount with her for supper, if they wouldn't let her stay the night. After Clementina had driven away, Mrs. Claxon accused herself to her husband of being the greatest fool in the State, but he said that the carriage was one of the Middlemount rigs, and he guessed it was all right. He could see that Clem was wild to go, and he didn't see why she shouldn't.

"Well, I do, then," his wife retorted. "We don't know anything about the woman, or who she is."

"I guess no harm'll come to Clem for one night," said Claxon, and Mrs. Claxon was forced back upon the larger question for the maintenance of her anxiety. She asked what he was going to do about letting Clem go the whole winter with a perfect stranger; and he answered that he had not got round to that yet, and that there were a good many things to be thought of first. He got round to see the rector before dark, and in the light of his larger horizon, was better able to orient Mrs. Lander and her motives than he had been before.

When she came back with the girl the next morning, she had thought of something in the nature of credentials. It was the letter from her church in Boston, which she took whenever she left home, so that if she wished she might unite with the church in any place where she happened to be stopping. It did not make a great impression upon the Klaxons, who were of no religion, though they allowed their children to go to the Episcopal church and Sunday-school, and always meant to go themselves. They said they would like to talk the matter over with the rector, if Mrs. Lander did not object; she offered to send her carriage for him, and the rector was brought at once.

He was one of those men who have, in the breaking down of the old Puritanical faith, and the dying out of the later Unitarian rationalism, advanced and established the Anglican church so notably in the New England hill-country, by a wise conformity to the necessities and exactions of the native temperament. On the ecclesiastical side he was conscientiously uncompromising, but personally he was as simple-mannered as he was simple-hearted. He was a tall lean man in rusty black, with a clerical waistcoat that buttoned high, and scholarly glasses, but with a belated straw hat that had counted more than one summer, and a farmer's tan on his face and hands. He pronounced the church-letter, though quite outside of his own church, a document of the highest respectability, and he listened with patient deference to the autobiography which Mrs. Lander poured out upon him, and her identifications, through reference to this or that person in Boston whom he knew either at first or second hand. He had not to pronounce upon her syntax, or her social quality; it was enough for him, in behalf of the Claxons, to find her what she professed to be.

"You must think," he said, laughing, "that we are over-particular; but the fact is that we value Clementina rather highly, and we wish to be sure that your hospitable offer will be for her real good."

"Of cou'se," said Mrs. Lander. "I should be just so myself abort her."

"I don't know," he continued, "that I've ever said how much we think of her, Mrs. Richling and I, but this seems a good opportunity, as she is not present.

"She is not perfect, but she comes as near being a thoroughly good girl as she can without knowing it. She has a great deal of common-sense, and we all want her to have the best chance."

"Well, that's just the way I feel about her, and that's just what I mean to give her," said Mrs. Lander.

"I am not sure that I make myself quite clear," said the rector. "I mean, a chance to prove how useful and helpful she can be. Do you think you can make life hard for her occasionally? Can you be peevish and exacting, and unreasonable? Can you do something to make her value superfluity and luxury at their true worth?"

Mrs. Lander looked a little alarmed and a little offended. "I don't know as I undastand what you mean, exactly," she said, frowning rather with perplexity than resentment. "But the child sha'n't have a care, and her own motha couldn't be betta to her than me. There a'n't anything money can buy that she sha'n't have, if she wants it, and all I'll ask of her is 't she'll enjoy herself as much as she knows how. I want her with me because I should love to have her round; and we did from the very fust minute she spoke, Mr. Lander and me, both. She shall have her own money, and spend it for anything she pleases, and she needn't do a stitch o' work from mohnin' till night. But if you're afraid I shall put upon her."

"No, no," said the rector, and he threw back his head with a laugh.

When it was all arranged, a few days later, after the verification of certain of Mrs. Lander's references by letters to Boston, he said to Clementina's father and mother, "There's only one danger, now, and that is that she will spoil Clementina; but there's a reasonable hope that she won't know how." He found the Claxons struggling with a fresh misgiving, which Claxon expressed. "The way I look at it is like this. I don't want that woman should eva think Clem was after her money. On the face of it there a'n't very much to her that would make anybody think but what we was after it; and I should want it pootty well undastood that we wa'n't that kind. But I don't seem to see any way of tellin' her."

"No," said the rector, with a sympathetic twinkle, "that would be difficult."

"It's plain to be seen," Mrs. Claxon interposed, "that she thinks a good deal of her money; and I d' know but what she'd think she was doin' Clem most too much of a favor anyway. If it can't be a puffectly even thing, all round, I d' know as I should want it to be at all."

"You're quite right, Mrs. Claxon, quite right. But I believe Mrs. Lander may be safely left to look out for her own interests. After all, she has merely asked Clementina to pass the winter with her. It will be a good opportunity for her to see something of the world; and perhaps it may bring her the chance of placing herself in life. We have got to consider these things with reference to a young girl."

Mrs. Claxon said, "Of cou'se," but Claxon did not assent so readily.

"I don't feel as if I should want Clem to look at it in that light. If the chance don't come to her, I don't want she should go huntin' round for it."

"I thoroughly agree with you," said the rector. "But I was thinking that there was not only no chance worthy of her in Middlemount, but there is no chance at all."

"I guess that's so," Claxon owned with a laugh. "Well, I guess we can leave it to Clem to do what's right and proper everyway. As you say, she's got lots of sense."

From that moment he emptied his mind of care concerning the matter; but husband and wife are never both quite free of care on the same point of common interest, and Mrs. Claxon assumed more and more of the anxieties which he had abandoned. She fretted under the load, and expressed an exasperated tenderness for Clementina when the girl seemed forgetful of any of the little steps to be taken before the great one in getting her clothes ready for leaving home. She said finally that she presumed they were doing a wild thing, and that it looked crazier and crazier the more she thought of it;

but all was, if Clem didn't like, she could come home. By this time her husband was in something of that insensate eagerness to have the affair over that people feel in a house where there is a funeral.

At the station, when Clementina started for Boston with Mrs. Lander, her father and mother, with the rector and his wife, came to see her off. Other friends mistakenly made themselves of the party, and kept her talking vacuities when her heart was full, till the train drew up. Her father went with her into the parlor car, where the porter of the Middlemount House set down Mrs. Lander's hand baggage and took the final fee she thrust upon him. When Claxon came out he was not so satisfactory about the car as he might have been to his wife, who had never been inside a parlor car, and who had remained proudly in the background, where she could not see into it from the outside. He said that he had felt so bad about Clem that he did not notice what the car was like. But he was able to report that she looked as well as any of the folks in it, and that, if there were any better dressed, he did not see them. He owned that she cried some, when he said good-bye to her.

"I guess," said his wife, grimly, "we're a passel o' fools to let her go. Even if she don't like, the'a, with that crazy-head, she won't be the same Clem when she comes back."

They were too heavy-hearted to dispute much, and were mostly silent as they drove home behind Claxon's self-broken colt: a creature that had taken voluntarily to harness almost from its birth, and was an example to its kind in sobriety and industry.

The children ran out from the house to meet them, with a story of having seen Clem at a point in the woods where the train always slowed up before a crossing, and where they had all gone to wait for her. She had seen them through the car-window, and had come out on the car platform, and waved her handkerchief, as she passed, and called something to them, but they could not hear what it was, they were all cheering so.

At this their mother broke down, and went crying into the house. Not to have had the last words of the child whom she should never see the same again if she ever saw her at all, was more, she said, than heart could bear.

The rector's wife arrived home with her husband in a mood of mounting hopefulness, which soared to tops commanding a view of perhaps more of this world's kingdoms than a clergyman's wife ought ever to see, even for another. She decided that Clementina's chances of making a splendid match, somewhere, were about of the nature of certainties, and she contended that she would adorn any station, with experience, and with her native tact, especially if it were a very high station in Europe, where Mrs. Lander would now be sure to take her. If she did not take her to Europe, however, she would be sure to leave her all her money, and this would serve the same end, though more indirectly.

Mr. Richling scoffed at this ideal of Clementina's future with a contempt which was as little becoming to his cloth. He made his wife reflect that, with all her inherent grace and charm, Clementina was an ignorant little country girl, who had neither the hardness of heart nor the greediness of soul, which gets people on in the world, and repair for them the disadvantages of birth and education. He represented that even if favorable chances for success in society showed themselves to the girl, the intense and inexpugnable vulgarity of Mrs. Lander would spoil them; and he was glad of this, he said, for he believed that the best thing which could happen to the child would be to come home as sweet and good as she had gone away; he added this was what they ought both to pray for.

His wife admitted this, but she retorted by asking if he thought such a thing was possible, and he was obliged to own that it was not possible. He marred the effect of his concession by subjoining that it was no more possible than her making a brilliant and triumphant social figure in society, either at home or in Europe.

XIII

So far from embarking at once for Europe, Mrs. Lander went to that hotel in a suburb of Boston, where she had the habit of passing the late autumn months, in order to fortify herself for the climate of the early winter months in the city. She was a little puzzled how to provide for Clementina, with respect to herself, but she decided that the best thing would be to have her sleep in a room opening out of her own, with a folding bed in it, so that it could be used as a sort of parlor for both of them during the day, and be within easy reach, for conversation, at all times.

On her part, Clementina began by looking after Mrs. Lander's comforts, large and little, like a daughter, to her own conception and to that of Mrs. Lander, but to other eyes, like a servant. Mrs. Lander shyly shrank from acquaintance among the other ladies, and in the absence of this, she could not introduce Clementina, who went down to an early breakfast alone, and sat apart with her at lunch and dinner, ministering to her in public as she did in private. She ran back to their rooms to fetch her shawl, or her handkerchief, or whichever drops or powders she happened to be taking with her meals, and adjusted with closer care the hassock which the head waiter had officially placed at her feet. They seldom sat in the parlor where the ladies met, after dinner; they talked only to each other; and there, as elsewhere, the girl kept her filial care of the old woman. The question of her relation to Mrs. Lander became so pressing among several of the guests that, after Clementina had watched over the banisters, with throbbing heart and feet, a little dance one night which the other girls had got up among themselves, and had fled back to her room at the approach of one of the kindlier and bolder of them, the landlord felt forced to learn from Mrs. Lander how Miss Claxon was to be regarded. He managed delicately, by saying he would give the Sunday paper she had ordered to her nurse, "Or, I beg your pardon," he added, as if he had made a mistake. "Why, she a'n't my nuhse," Mrs. Lander explained, simply, neither annoyed nor amused; "she's just a young lady that's visiting me, as you may say," and this put an end to the misgiving among the ladies. But it suggested something to Mrs. Lander, and a few days afterwards, when they came out from Boston where they had been shopping, and she had been lavishing a bewildering waste of gloves, hats, shoes, capes and gowns upon Clementina, she said, "I'll tell you what. We've got to have a maid."

"A maid?" cried the girl.

"It isn't me, or my things I want her for," said Mrs. Lander. "It's you and these dresses of youas. I presume you could look afta them, come to give youa mind to it; but I don't want to have you tied up to a lot of clothes; and I presume we should find her a comfo't in moa ways than one, both of us. I don't know what we shall want her to do, exactly; but I guess she will, if she undastands her business, and I want you should go in with me, to-morror, and find one. I'll speak to some of the ladies, and find out whe's the best place to go, and we'll get the best there is."

A lady whom Mrs. Lander spoke to entered into the affair with zeal born of a lurking sense of the wrong she had helped do Clementina in the common doubt whether she was not herself Mrs. Lander's maid. She offered to go into Boston with them to an intelligence office, where you could get nice girls of all kinds; but she ended by giving Mrs. Lander the address, and instructions as to what she was to require in a maid. She was chiefly to get an English maid, if at all possible, for the qualifications would more or less naturally follow from her nationality. There proved to be no English maid, but there was a Swedish one who had received a rigid training in an English family living on the Continent, and had come immediately from that service to seek her first place in America. The manager of the office pronounced her character, as set down in writing, faultless, and Mrs. Lander engaged her. "You want to look afta this young lady," she said, indicating Clementina. "I can look afta myself," but Ellida took charge of them both on the train out from Boston with prompt intelligence.

"We got to get used to it, I guess," Mrs. Lander confided at the first chance of whispering to Clementina.

Within a month after washing the faces and combing the hair of all her brothers and sisters who would suffer it at her hands, Clementina's own head was under the brush of a lady's maid, who was of as great a discreetness in her own way as Clementina herself. She supplied the defects of Mrs. Lander's elementary habits by simply asking if she should get this thing and that thing for the toilet, without criticising its absence, - and then asking whether she should get the same things for her young lady. She appeared to let Mrs. Lander decide between having her brushes in ivory or silver, but there was really no choice for her, and they came in silver. She knew not only her own place, but the places of her two ladies, and she presently had them in such training that they were as proficient in what they might and might not do for themselves and for each other, as if making these distinctions were the custom of their lives.

Their hearts would both have gone out to Ellida, but Ellida kept them at a distance with the smooth respectfulness of the iron hand in the glove of velvet; and Clementina first learned from her to imagine the impassable gulf between mistress and maid.

At the end of her month she gave them, out of a clear sky, a week's warning. She professed no grievance, and was not moved by Mrs. Lander's appeal to say what wages she wanted.

She would only say that she was going to take a place an Commonwealth Avenue, where a friend of hers was living, and when the week was up, she went, and left her late mistresses feeling rather blank. "I presume we shall have to get anotha," said Mrs. Lander.

"Oh, not right away!" Clementina pleaded.

"Well, not right away," Mrs. Lander assented; and provisionally they each took the other into her keeping, and were much freer and happier together.

Soon after Clementina was startled one morning, as she was going in to breakfast, by seeing Mr. Fane at the clerk's desk. He did not see her; he was looking down at the hotel register, to compute the bill of a departing guest; but when she passed out she found him watching for her, with some letters.

"I didn't know you were with us," he said, with his pensive smile, "till I found your letters here, addressed to Mrs. Lander's care; and then I put two and two together. It only shows how small the world is, don't you think so? I've just got back from my vacation; I prefer to take it in the fall of the year, because it's so much pleasanter to travel, then. I suppose you didn't know I was here?"

"No, I didn't," said Clementina. "I never dreamed of such a thing."

"To be sure; why should you?" Fane reflected. "I've been here ever since last spring. But I'll say this, Miss Claxon, that if it's the least unpleasant to you, or the least disagreeable, or awakens any kind of associations -"

"Oh, no!" Clementina protested, and Fane was spared the pain of saying what he would do if it were.

He bowed, and she said sweetly, "It's pleasant to meet any one I've seen before. I suppose you don't know how much it's changed at Middlemount since you we' e thea." Fane answered blankly, while he felt in his breast pocket, Oh, he presumed so; and she added: "Ha'dly any of the same guests came back this summer, and they had more in July than they had in August, Mrs. Atwell said. Mr. Mahtin, the chef, is gone, and newly all the help is different."

Fane kept feeling in one pocket and then slapped himself over the other pockets. "No," he said, "I haven't got it with me. I must have left it in my room. I just received a letter from Frank - Mr. Gregory, you know, I always call him Frank - and I thought I had it with me. He was asking about Middlemount; and I wanted to read you what he said. But I'll find it upstairs. He's out of college, now, and he's begun his studies in the divinity school. He's at Andover. I don't know what to make of Frank, oftentimes," the clerk continued, confidentially. "I tell him he's a kind of a survival, in religion; he's so aesthetic." It seemed to Fane that he had not meant aesthetic, exactly, but he could not ask Clementina what the word was. He went on to say, "He's a grand good fellow, Frank is, but he don't make enough allowance for human nature. He's more like one of those old fashioned orthodox. I go in for having a good time, so long as you don't do anybody else any hurt."

He left her, and went to receive the commands of a lady who was leaning over the desk, and saying severely, "My mail, if you please," and Clementina could not wait for him to come back; she had to go to Mrs. Lander, and get her ready for breakfast; Ellida had taught Mrs. Lander a luxury of helplessness in which she persisted after the maid's help was withdrawn.

Clementina went about the whole day with the wonder what Gregory had said about Middlemount filling her mind. It must have had something to do with her; he could not have forgotten the words he had asked her to forget. She remembered them now with a curiosity, which had no rancor in it, to know why he really took them back. She had never blamed him, and she had outlived the hurt she had felt at not hearing from him. But she had never lost the hope of hearing from him, or rather the expectation, and now she found that she was eager for his message; she decided that it must be something like a message, although it could not be anything direct. No one else had come to his place in her fancy, and she was willing to try what they would think of each other now, to measure her own obligation to the past by a knowledge of his. There was scarcely more than this in her heart when she allowed herself to drift near Fane's place that night, that he might speak to her, and tell her what Gregory had said. But he had apparently forgotten about his letter, and only wished to talk about himself. He wished to analyze himself, to tell her what sort of person he was. He dealt impartially with the subject; he did not spare some faults of his; and after a week, he proposed a correspondence with her, in a letter of carefully studied spelling, as a means of mutual improvement as well as further acquaintance.

It cost Clementina a good deal of trouble to answer him as she wished and not hurt his feelings. She declined in terms she thought so cold that they must offend him beyond the point of speaking to her again; but he sought her out, as soon after as he could, and thanked her for her kindness, and begged her pardon. He said he knew that she was a very busy person, with all the lessons she was taking, and that she had no time for carrying on a correspondence. He regretted that he could not write French, because then the correspondence would have been good practice for her. Clementina had begun taking French lessons, of a teacher who came out from Boston. She lunched three times a week with her and Mrs. Lander, and spoke the language with Clementina, whose accent she praised for its purity; purity of accent was characteristic of all this lady's pupils; but what was really extraordinary in Mademoiselle Claxon was her sense of grammatical structure; she wrote the language even more perfectly than she spoke it; but beautifully, but wonderfully; her exercises were something marvellous.

Mrs. Lander would have liked Clementina to take all the lessons that she heard any of the other young ladies in the hotel were taking. One of them went in town every day, and studied drawing at an art-school, and she wanted Clementina to do that, too. But Clementina would not do that; she had tried often enough at home, when her brother Jim was drawing, and her father was designing the patterns of his woodwork; she knew that she never could do it, and the time would be wasted. She decided against piano lessons and singing lessons, too; she did not care for either, and she pleaded that it would be a waste to study them; but she suggested dancing lessons, and her gift for dancing won greater praise, and perhaps sincerer, than her accent won from Mademoiselle Blanc, though Mrs. Lander said that she would not have believed any one could be more complimentary. She learned the new steps and figures in all the fashionable dances; she mastered some fancy dances, which society was then beginning to borrow from the stage; and she gave these before Mrs. Lander with a success which she felt herself.

"I believe I could teach dancing," she said.

"Well, you won't eve' haf to, child," returned Mrs. Lander, with an eye on the side of the case that seldom escaped her.

In spite of his wish to respect these preoccupations, Fane could not keep from offering Clementina attentions, which took the form of persecution when they changed from flowers for Mrs. Lander's table to letters for herself. He apologized for his letters whenever he met her; but at last one of them came to her before breakfast with a special delivery stamp from Boston. He had withdrawn to the city to write it, and he said that if she could not make him a favorable answer, he should not come back to Woodlake.

She had to show this letter to Mrs. Lander, who asked: "You want he should come back?"

"No, indeed! I don't want eva to see him again."

"Well, then, I guess you'll know how to tell him so."

The girl went into her own room to write, and when she brought her answer to show it to Mrs. Lander she found her in frowning thought. "I don't know but you'll have to go back and write it all over again, Clementina," she said, "if you've told him not to come. I've been thinkin', if you don't want to have anything to do with him, we betta go ouaselves."

"Yes," answered Clementina, "that's what I've said."

"You have? Well, the witch is in it! How came you to -"

"I just wanted to talk with you about it. But I thought maybe you'd like to go. Or at least I should. I should like to go home, Mrs. Landa."

"Home!" retorted Mrs. Lander. "The'e's plenty of places where you can be safe from the fella besides home, though I'll take you back the'a this minute if you say so. But you needn't to feel wo'ked up about it."

"Oh, I'm not," said Clementina, but with a gulp which betrayed her nervousness.

"I did think," Mrs. Lander went on, "that I should go into the Vonndome, for December and January, but just as likely as not he'd come pesterin' the'a, too, and I wouldn't go, now, if you was to give me the whole city of Boston. Why shouldn't we go to Florid?"

When Mrs. Lander had once imagined the move, the nomadic impulse mounted irresistably in her. She spoke of hotels in the South, where they could renew the summer, and she mapped out a campaign which she put into instant action so far as to advance upon New York.

Choose from Thousands of 1stWorldLibrary Classics By

A. M. Barnard	C. M. Ingleby	Elizabeth Gaskell
Ada Leverson	Carolyn Wells	Elizabeth McCracken
Adolphus William Ward	Catherine Parr Traill	Elizabeth Von Arnim
Aesop	Charles A. Eastman	Ellem Key
Agatha Christie	Charles Amory Beach	Emerson Hough
Alexander Aaronsohn	Charles Dickens	Emilie F. Carlen
Alexander Kielland	Charles Dudley Warner	Emily Dickinson
Alexandre Dumas	Charles Farrar Browne	Enid Bagnold
Alfred Gatty	Charles Ives	Enilor Macartney Lane
Alfred Ollivant	Charles Kingsley	Erasmus W. Jones
Alice Duer Miller	Charles Klein	Ernie Howard Pie
Alice Turner Curtis	Charles Hanson Towne	Ethel May Dell
Alice Dunbar	Charles Lathrop Pack	Ethel Turner
Allen Chapman	Charles Romyn Dake	Ethel Watts Mumford
Ambrose Bierce	Charles Whibley	Eugenie Foa
Amelia E. Barr	Charles Willing Beale	Eugene Wood
Amory H. Bradford	Charlotte M. Braeme	Eustace Hale Ball
Andrew Lang	Charlotte M. Yonge	Evelyn Everett-green
Andrew McFarland Davis	Charlotte Perkins Stetson	Everard Cotes
Andy Adams	Clair W. Hayes	F. H. Cheley
Anna Alice Chapin	Clarence Day Jr.	F. J. Cross
Anna Sewell	Clarence E. Mulford	F. Marion Crawford
Annie Besant	Clemence Housman	Federick Austin Ogg
Annie Hamilton Donnell	Confucius	Ferdinand Ossendowski
Annie Payson Call	Coningsby Dawson	Francis Bacon
Annie Roe Carr	Cornelis DeWitt Wilcox	Francis Darwin
Annonaymous	Cyril Burleigh	Frances Hodgson Burnett
Anton Chekhov	D. H. Lawrence	Frances Parkinson Keyes
Arnold Bennett	Daniel Defoe	Frank Gee Patchin
Arthur Conan Doyle	David Garnett	Frank Harris
Arthur M. Winfield	Dinah Craik	Frank Jewett Mather
Arthur Ransome	Don Carlos Janes	Frank L. Packard
Arthur Schnitzler	Donald Keyhoe	Frank V. Webster
Atticus	Dorothy Kilner	Frederic Stewart Isham
B.H. Baden-Powell	Dougan Clark	Frederick Trevor Hill
B. M. Bower	Douglas Fairbanks	Frederick Winslow Taylor
B. C. Chatterjee	E. Nesbit	Friedrich Kerst
Baroness Emmuska Orczy	E.P.Roe	Friedrich Nietzsche
Baroness Orczy	E. Phillips Oppenheim	Fyodor Dostoyevsky
Basil King	Earl Barnes	G.A. Henty
Bayard Taylor	Edgar Rice Burroughs	G.K. Chesterton
Ben Macomber	Edith Van Dyne	Gabrielle E. Jackson
Bertha Muzzy Bower	Edith Wharton	Garrett P. Serviss
Bjornstjerne Bjornson	Edward Everett Hale	Gaston Leroux
Booth Tarkington	Edward J. O'Biren	George A. Warren
Boyd Cable	Edward S. Ellis	George Ade
Bram Stoker	Edwin L. Arnold	Geroge Bernard Shaw
C. Collodi	Eleanor Atkins	George Durston
C. E. Orr	Eliot Gregory	George Ebers

George Eliot
George Gissing
George MacDonald
George Meredith
George Orwell
George Sylvester Viereck
George Tucker
George W. Cable
George Wharton James
Gertrude Atherton
Gordon Casserly
Grace E. King
Grace Gallatin
Grace Greenwood
Grant Allen
Guillermo A. Sherwell
Gulielma Zollinger
Gustav Flaubert
H. A. Cody
H. B. Irving
H.C. Bailey
H. G. Wells
H. H. Munro
H. Irving Hancock
H. Rider Haggard
H. W. C. Davis
Haldeman Julius
Hall Caine
Hamilton Wright Mabie
Hans Christian Andersen
Harold Avery
Harold McGrath
Harriet Beecher Stowe
Harry Castlemon
Harry Coghill
Harry Houdini
Hayden Carruth
Helent Hunt Jackson
Helen Nicolay
Hendrik Conscience
Hendy David Thoreau
Henri Barbusse
Henrik Ibsen
Henry Adams
Henry Ford
Henry Frost
Henry James
Henry Jones Ford
Henry Seton Merriman
Henry W Longfellow
Herbert A. Giles

Herbert Carter
Herbert N. Casson
Herman Hesse
Hildegard G. Frey
Homer
Honore De Balzac
Horace B. Day
Horace Walpole
Horatio Alger Jr.
Howard Pyle
Howard R. Garis
Hugh Lofting
Hugh Walpole
Humphry Ward
Ian Maclaren
Inez Haynes Gillmore
Irving Bacheller
Isabel Hornibrook
Israel Abrahams
Ivan Turgenev
J.G.Austin
J. Henri Fabre
J. M. Barrie
J. Macdonald Oxley
J. S. Fletcher
J. S. Knowles
J. Storer Clouston
Jack London
Jacob Abbott
James Allen
James Andrews
James Baldwin
James Branch Cabell
James DeMille
James Joyce
James Lane Allen
James Lane Allen
James Oliver Curwood
James Oppenheim
James Otis
James R. Driscoll
Jane Austen
Jane L. Stewart
Janet Aldridge
Jens Peter Jacobsen
Jerome K. Jerome
John Burroughs
John Cournos
John F. Kennedy
John Gay
John Glasworthy

John Habberton
John Joy Bell
John Kendrick Bangs
John Milton
John Philip Sousa
Jonas Lauritz Idemil Lie
Jonathan Swift
Joseph A. Altsheler
Joseph Carey
Joseph Conrad
Joseph E. Badger Jr
Joseph Hergesheimer
Joseph Jacobs
Jules Vernes
Julian Hawthrone
Julie A Lippmann
Justin Huntly McCarthy
Kakuzo Okakura
Kenneth Grahame
Kenneth McGaffey
Kate Langley Bosher
Kate Langley Bosher
Katherine Cecil Thurston
Katherine Stokes
L. A. Abbot
L. T. Meade
L. Frank Baum
Latta Griswold
Laura Dent Crane
Laura Lee Hope
Laurence Housman
Lawrence Beasley
Leo Tolstoy
Leonid Andreyev
Lewis Carroll
Lewis Sperry Chafer
Lilian Bell
Lloyd Osbourne
Louis Hughes
Louis Tracy
Louisa May Alcott
Lucy Fitch Perkins
Lucy Maud Montgomery
Luther Benson
Lydia Miller Middleton
Lyndon Orr
M. Corvus
M. H. Adams
Margaret E. Sangster
Margret Howth
Margaret Vandercook

Margret Penrose	Rex E. Beach	Thomas H. Huxley
Maria Edgeworth	Richard Harding Davis	Thomas Hardy
Maria Thompson Daviess	Richard Jefferies	Thomas More
Mariano Azuela	Richard Le Gallienne	Thornton W. Burgess
Marion Polk Angellotti	Robert Barr	U. S. Grant
Mark Overton	Robert Frost	Valentine Williams
Mark Twain	Robert Gordon Anderson	Various Authors
Mary Austin	Robert L. Drake	Vaughan Kester
Mary Catherine Crowley	Robert Lansing	Victor Appleton
Mary Cole	Robert Lynd	Victoria Cross
Mary Hastings Bradley	Robert Michael Ballantyne	Virginia Woolf
Mary Roberts Rinehart	Robert W. Chambers	Wadsworth Camp
Mary Rowlandson	Rosa Nouchette Carey	Walter Camp
M. Wollstonecraft Shelley	Rudyard Kipling	Walter Scott
Maud Lindsay	Samuel B. Allison	Washington Irving
Max Beerbohm	Samuel Hopkins Adams	Wilbur Lawton
Myra Kelly	Sarah Bernhardt	Wilkie Collins
Nathaniel Hawthrone	Sarah C. Hallowell	Willa Cather
Nicolo Machiavelli	Selma Lagerlof	Willard F. Baker
O. F. Walton	Sherwood Anderson	William Dean Howells
Oscar Wilde	Sigmund Freud	William le Queux
Owen Johnson	Standish O'Grady	W. Makepeace Thackeray
P.G. Wodehouse	Stanley Weyman	William W. Walter
Paul and Mabel Thorne	Stella Benson	William Shakespeare
Paul G. Tomlinson	Stella M. Francis	Winston Churchill
Paul Severing	Stephen Crane	Yei Theodora Ozaki
Percy Brebner	Stewart Edward White	Yogi Ramacharaka
Peter B. Kyne	Stijn Streuvels	Young E. Allison
Plato	Swami Abhedananda	Zane Grey
R. Derby Holmes	Swami Parmananda	
R. L. Stevenson	T. S. Ackland	
R. S. Ball	T. S. Arthur	
Rabindranath Tagore	The Princess Der Ling	
Rahul Alvares	Thomas A. Janvier	
Ralph Bonehill	Thomas A Kempis	
Ralph Henry Barbour	Thomas Anderton	
Ralph Victor	Thomas Bailey Aldrich	
Ralph Waldo Emmerson	Thomas Bulfinch	
Rene Descartes	Thomas De Quincey	
Rex Beach	Thomas Dixon	

www.ingramcontent.com/pod-product-compliance
Lightning Source LLC
Chambersburg PA
CBHW021917160426
42813CB00104B/3138/J